CONTEMPORARY WRITERS

General Editors
MALCOLM BRADBURY
and
CHRISTOPHER BIGSBY

NADINE GORDIMER

NADINE
GORDIMER

JUDIE NEWMAN

ROUTLEDGE
LONDON AND NEW YORK

First published in 1988 by
Routledge
11 New Fetter Lane, London EC4P 4EE
29 West 35th Street, New York NY 10001

© 1988 Judie Newman

Photoset by Rowland Phototypesetting Ltd
Printed in Great Britain by Cox & Wyman Ltd, Reading

British Library Cataloguing in Publication Data
Newman, Judie
Nadine Gordimer. – (Contemporary writers).
1. Fiction in English. South African writers.
Gordimer, Nadine, 1923–
I. Title   II. Series
823

0-415-00660-0

Library of Congress Cataloging in Publication Data
Newman, Judie
Nadine Gordimer.
(Contemporary writers)
Bibliography: p.
Includes index
1. Gordimer, Nadine – Criticism and interpretation.
I. Title   II. Series
PR9369.3.G3Z79   1988   823   88-11492

ISBN 0-415-00660-0 (pbk.)

In memory of my grandmother
Emily May Cross
1901–1984

CONTENTS

GENERAL EDITORS' PREFACE

The contemporary is a country which we all inhabit, but there is little agreement as to its boundaries or its shape. The serious writer is one of its most sensitive interpreters, but criticism is notoriously cautious in offering a response or making a judgement. Accordingly, this continuing series is an endeavour to look at some of the most important writers of our time, and the questions raised by their work. It is, in effect, an attempt to map the contemporary, to describe its aesthetic and moral topography.

The series came into existence out of two convictions. One was that, despite all the modern pressures on the writer and on literary culture, we live in a major creative time, as vigorous and alive in its distinctive way as any that went before. The other was that, though criticism itself tends to grow more theoretical and apparently indifferent to contemporary creation, there are grounds for a lively aesthetic debate. This series, which includes books written from various standpoints, is meant to provide a forum for that debate. By design, some of those who have contributed are themselves writers, willing to respond to their contemporaries; others are critics who have brought to the discussion of current writing the spirit of contemporary criticism or simply a conviction, forcibly and coherently argued, for the contemporary significance of their subjects. Our aim, as the series develops, is to continue to explore the works of major post-war writers – in fiction, drama and poetry – over an international range, and thereby to illuminate not only those works but also in some degree the artistic, social and moral assumptions on which they rest. Our wish is that, in their very variety of approach and emphasis, these books will stimulate interest in and understanding of the vitality of a living literature which, because it is contemporary, is especially ours.

Norwich, England . MALCOLM BRADBURY
CHRISTOPHER BIGSBY

PREFACE AND ACKNOWLEDGEMENTS

The author and publisher wish to thank the following for permission to quote copyright material: Jonathan Cape Ltd; Russell and Volkening, Inc. I am also grateful to the editors of *Critique: Studies in Modern Fiction* (1981), *Journal of Commonwealth Literature* (1985), and *Third World Quarterly* (1987) for the opportunity to publish pilot versions of parts of chapters 3, 4, and 5. I gratefully acknowledge the assistance of the Small Grants Sub-Committee of the University of Newcastle-upon-Tyne, which enabled me to undertake research in other libraries, and of the staff of the National Library of Scotland, and the Library of the University of Newcastle-upon-Tyne, especially Lynette Bomford, and the staff of the Inter-Library Loans Department, for speedy assistance in obtaining bibliographical material. Special thanks are also due to Alison Gallagher, Margaret Jones, and Kathleen O'Rawe for secretarial assistance. Within the scope of a short study I could not aspire to take issue with, or even to cite, the wealth of secondary criticism of Gordimer's works, but I have certainly learned from it all. Many people have helped with information, documentation and criticism; my gratitude goes particularly to my colleagues and students in Newcastle, and specifically to Linda Anderson, Mary Bill, Stephen Clingman, Jenny Dawe, Derek Green, Robert Green, Thami Mseleku, Hermann Moisl, Paul Rich, and David Rycroft. Finally I should like to thank Ian, Christopher, and Ivy Revie, who contributed their time, energy, and moral support, and my parents Cash and Alice Newman, who will understand why this book is dedicated to the memory of my grandmother, Emily May Cross.

In the context of apartheid, entering into the minutiae of terminological choice is akin to the selection of a necktie for a throat cancer. Throughout this study the terms 'black', 'white', and 'coloured' are employed to refer to the arbitrary racial categorizations imposed by the government of South Africa upon the people of that country. I hope it will become clear that this in no way implies acceptance of their ideological implications.

A NOTE ON THE TEXTS

Page references for quotations from Nadine Gordimer's novels are taken from the British (Jonathan Cape) editions.

1

INTRODUCTION

Writing in 1980 Gordimer raised the fundamental question of South African fiction: 'Who is qualified to write about whom?'.[1] As a white writer, Gordimer's fictional enterprise involves a refusal to exercise white proxy in the arts, but rather to seek out narrative forms which combine European and indigenous cultures and are attentive to the majority voice in South Africa. As a result her work is both politically committed and formally innovative, involving subject matter of intense contemporary interest, to which Gordimer has responded with a multiplicity of narrative strategies. Major concerns in her work include racism, the crisis of Liberal values, the nature of the historical consciousness, and sexual politics. While Gordimer operates within a divided society, and must be understood within her South African context, her writing also offers an important contribution to the postmodernist reassessment of narrative poetics, and a conscious challenge to European conceptions of the novel. Gordimer is, of course, also prolific in other forms, the author of essays, literary criticism, and some two hundred short stories, and a collaborator in photographic studies and work for television. The short stories in particular deserve a study of their own. In order to avoid introducing distraction by a summary treatment of Gordimer's work in other genres, the present volume concentrates upon the novels. Only a reading which respects the precise specificities of narrative structure can hope to indicate the subtlety with which Gordimer subverts Eurocentric conventions. Individual novels pose the question 'Whose story is it?' quite variously: by establishing a counterpoint between male and female protagonist, white and black interpreters; by employing double plots which readjust the relation between social context, text, and subtext; by the reconstruction of the implied reader; and by interrogating the linguistics of the South African cultural voice.

What of the storyteller herself? Gordimer was born in Springs, a small mining town on Johannesburg's East Rand, in 1923, the daughter of a Jewish jeweller and a mother of British descent. She has described her father as lacking a strong personality, almost as if burnt out by his experience of pogroms and persecution, and by the effort involved in bringing nine sisters out of Lithuania. In contrast Gordimer's mother was a dominating influence in one vital respect at least. When Gordimer was 10 years old, a sudden faint led to the diagnosis of an over-rapid heartbeat. Her mother promptly forbade all physical activity, including dancing, which Gordimer passionately enjoyed, eventually removing the child from school altogether. The years between 11 and 16 passed in intense loneliness, without any contact with other children. Later, Gordimer discovered that her 'heart problem' was a fiction, unconsciously fostered by her unhappily married mother, to promote her own emotional needs. Before her mother's death Gordimer suppressed these facts from early autobiographical writings. Interviewed in 1983 she commented that 'It's really only in the last decade of my life that I've been able to face all this'.[2] The suspicion lingers that it was this experience which made Gordimer into a novelist. The years spent in solitude, reading anything and everything, gave extra impetus to an interest in writing initiated at the age of 9, somewhat improbably, with a poem eulogising Paul Kruger. After publishing short stories for children, the 15-year-old writer saw her first adult story accepted by *The Forum*, one of many Liberal South African magazines to publish her early work. Through the intervention of the Afrikaans poet, Uys

Krige, American journals (the *New Yorker* and *Yale Review*) swiftly followed suit, until with a collection of stories published in 1949 and a novel in 1953, an international literary career was under way. In her own country Gordimer has received the backhanded compliment of seeing three of her novels banned. Elsewhere, as the recipient of such major literary awards as the James Tait Black Memorial Prize, the Booker Prize and the Grand Aigle D'Or, she is recognized as one of the most distinguished of contemporary novelists. When Jonathan Cape reissued her early novels, from 1976 to 1978, her readership expanded to the extent that today all her novels are in paperback, and also widely translated. As a frequent contributor to the *New York Review of Books* and the *New Yorker*, Gordimer has access to a discriminating international audience for whom her literary reputation is indisputable.

Importantly Gordimer has always disclaimed any specific political affiliation, adamantly insisting upon the primacy of her commitment to her writing. Uncomfortable at the prospect of finding herself caught in any orthodoxy, even of opposition, she has frequently expressed her unwillingness to become the subject of a moral rather than a literary judgement. Nonetheless it would be misleading to create the impression that she has merely observed South African political events impassively from the comfort of her study. Despite an implicitly aestheticist creed, Gordimer recognized in 1965 that apartheid had been the crucial experience of her life. In this connection two of her often reiterated statements speak for themselves: 'If you write honestly about life in South Africa, apartheid damns itself.' 'People like myself have two births, and the second one comes when you break out of the colour bar.'

Gordimer's own second birth appears to have coincided with the brief golden age of multiracialism associated with Sophiatown in the 1950s, when her involvement with *Drum* magazine brought her into contact with a large group of black writers, critics, and artists. It was the period later described by Gordimer as that of the 'Toy Telephone': groups and committees were talking everywhere about what needed to be done for

15

blacks, but nobody was listening at the other end. Sharpeville, the 1960 Treason Trial, the State of Emergency, the arrest and imprisonment of Nelson Mandela, the Rivonia trial of 1963, all issued in a period of unprecedented repression of both Liberal and radical protest. By the mid-1960s Gordimer's friends from that previous decade – Es'kia Mphahlele, Lewis Nkosi, Can Themba, and Nat Nakasa – had all left South Africa. In reaction to the silencing of an entire generation of black writers, Gordimer began a concerted campaign against censorship, linking political and cultural repression in a battery of essays and speeches. *The Black Interpreters*, a study of indigenous African writing, was one product of her championship of black writers.

With the rise of Black Consciousness in the 1970s, however, whites themselves were silenced in a different sense, increasingly sidelined as irrelevant by black activists intent on seizing their destiny in their own hands. The painful experience of marginalization extended into the arts. The multiracial writers' association in which Gordimer was active dissolved, with black writers forming their own group. Gordimer has publicly accepted the necessity for whites to play a role in South Africa only on black terms. Recently she welcomed the black trade union movement as providing one of the few areas where whites could work *with* rather than patronizingly *for* blacks. Throughout the 1970s Gordimer grew increasingly radical and now describes herself as a socialist in her general outlook.

While Gordimer's life and works display a steady politicization, her literary reception has undergone shifts of focus. Heralded at first for her acute, almost lyrical sensitivity, richness of style and precision of notational detail, Gordimer also attracted some hostile criticism. Typically reviewers commented adversely on her lack of narrative muscle, and on the coolness with which she treated themes which were perceived as essentially private. As detachment fell away, however, attention focused on Gordimer's ability to sustain a tense dialectic between the personal and the political. The two most recent

16

critical studies concentrate respectively on the different formative factors in Gordimer's life. Stephen Clingman reads her work largely in terms of the conditioning force of South Africa, situating her novels in relation to social and ideological codes and charting their response to the history of their society. John Cooke, in contrast, emphasizes the unusual childhood as a decisive influence, noting the recurrent motif of the possessive mother, and suggesting that Gordimer has endowed her private history with public associations, notably in the proposition that complete liberation from familial restraints requires a challenge to the dominant political order. Both are legitimate readings, distinguished by sophisticated critical acumen. Neither, however, makes enough of another conditioning factor, that of gender. Arguably, despite Gordimer's frequent contention that any feminist activity must remain subsidiary to the struggle against apartheid, she may be perceived as doubly marginalized in South Africa, as a white and as a woman. In her novels, the interaction of private and public, the complex investigation of the connection between psychological and political, draws upon an awareness of the relation of genre to gender.

THE LYING DAYS

Finding a genre is very much the major concern of Gordimer's early novels. If South Africa, like many colonial cultures, lacks a genre of its own, the same is true of Helen Shaw, the heroine of *The Lying Days*. Initially Helen perceives her existence as peripheral to European experience. Her childhood reading, tales of the ordinary adventures of English children, is entirely exotic to her: 'I had never read a book in which I myself was recognisable' (p. 20). Even novels with African settings are unfamiliar evocations of savage tribes, jungles, and elephants. While this theme of Eurocentric cultural dominance is more fully explored in *A World of Strangers*, in *The Lying Days* it is dwarfed by the formative influence of gender. As a *Bildungsroman* the novel invites a reading emphasizing the egocentricity of that form.[3] Recent theorizations of the female *Bildungsroman*,[4] however, have challenged the Hegelian assumption of the ultimate social complicity of the genre, recognizing that the nature of *Bildung* is itself problematic for women in a patriarchal culture. Typically, novels of female formation substitute inner concentration, a voyage in, for active rebellion, withdrawal or accommodation, employing episodic narrative structures to propose an alternative generic model. In any context development is a relative concept, involving such interrelated factors as class, history, gender, and race. As a South African female *Bildungsroman*, *The Lying Days* is carefully designed to offer the complexity of form necessary to represent these interrelationships, without falsifying, in an overcoherent narrative, the discontinuous *Bildung*, the underdevelopment of its heroine.

The novel opens with an emblematic sequence, as the young Helen, sulkily refusing to accompany her parents to their club, finds the refrain 'Not going anywhere' (p. 15) singing in her ears. To a child's question, 'Where you going' (p. 17) she shouts, 'Somewhere', setting off for the African stores. On arrival she notices a white boy, confidently 'finding his way about his own house' (p. 21), moving easily through the mine 'boys'. His existence startles Helen: 'He seemed to flash through my mind, tearing mystery, strangeness, as a thick cobweb splits to nothing brushed away by the hand of a man' (p. 21). While the young male freely enters the stores, Helen remains an outside observer, eventually fleeing back to parental security when she sees a mine 'boy' urinating. In little, the episode prefigures the problems inherent in 'going somewhere' for a character who is excluded from both the African world and that of the male.

Helen's incipient rebellion against the materialist values of her parents is also articulated through the (ludicrously phallic) figure of Ludi Koch, with whom her sexual awakening occurs. Ludi's nonconformity to bourgeois aspirations is overt. He refuses to 'get on' (p. 57) in the career sense. Indeed when a broken bridge prevents him physically from getting ahead, he leaps at the chance of an extended military leave, to enjoy an erotic idyll with Helen. Helen's original rejection of a university place reflects Ludi's influence, as she mentally envisages his ironic comment on such a step: 'Getting on, the bright ambitious daughter of the Mine Secretary' (p. 91). Later, at university, Helen meets Joel Aaron, in whose home she observes two photographs of his grandparents, the one a Talmudic scholar, 'a foolish man in the guise of a patriarch' (p. 113), the other expressing the 'real presence' of a woman, presiding over the room. Subsequently Helen learns that the family always overvalued the bookish male, whereas the grandmother was the 'go-getter' (p. 118) and economic mainstay. The juxtaposed images associate books with a patriarchal facade of power, bourgeois aspirations with the female, thus articulating the impasse between male and female, literary and economic paradigms, in which Helen finds herself. Another conditioning factor, that of race, surfaces in the character of Mary Seswayo, a black student whom Helen befriends. Helen first encounters Mary as a reflection in a cloakroom mirror, catching at the similarity between their expressions (p. 105). Like Helen's, Mary's education is hampered by the lack of a cultural context. As a Mission African, her idea of the white world is almost as bookish as Helen's, based on 'the Standard Six reader and Galilee nearly two thousand years ago' (p. 134). The narcissism of Helen's one-sided identification with Mary, however, is indicated when she encounters the poverty of the location where Mary lives, recognizing 'how useless it must all seem, how impossible to grasp, the structure of the English novel, the meaning of meaning, . . . with the woman making mealie porridge over the fire' (p. 187).

Though Helen's naive attempt to provide study facilities for Mary in her mother's home fails, the ensuing row catapults her from the parental world to a home with the Liberal Marcuses. It proves, however, a retrogressive step. The Marcuses figure as surrogate parents: John addresses Helen as 'good girl' (p. 210) and Jenny is first encountered breast-feeding, an iconic representation of motherhood. When Paul Clark appears, he jokingly identifies Helen with the Marcus baby: 'It's grown up awfully quickly' (p. 214). In her affair with Paul, Helen attempts to live 'in the greatest possible intimacy' (p. 251), refusing 'to belong to the women's camp while my husband belonged to the men's camp' (p. 251). Yet there are ominous signs that Paul prefers a world of separate gender spheres. As Helen struggles with an essay on George Eliot, Paul patronizes her: 'What's addling your little brain?' (p. 240), and attempts to cheer her up by sharing his hilarity at a black man's rejection of his wife as 'a damned ugly woman' (p. 241). For all his Liberal activities on behalf of Poor Relief, Paul enjoys cameraderie with the black male only in denigrating the female. From a surrogate family, Helen also moves to surrogate writing, abandoning her own studies in order to type Paul's thesis, agonizing over its syntax 'as if it were a piece of literature' (p. 247). When Paul complains, 'Helen, you're becoming a rotten wife' (p. 285) (his meal is late) she recognizes that her flight from conventional sexual paradigms has merely brought her full circle, 'cooking a man's breakfast and keeping my mouth shut' (p. 314).

A vestigial political parallel emerges in the conjunction of the failure of Paul and Helen's affair with the Nationalist victory of 1948 which paves the way for the Mixed Marriages Act. Haunted by Paul's description of mixed-race couples arrested in bed, dazzled by police torches, Helen awakes to car headlights in the bedroom and instinctively recoils from Paul (p. 261). The attempt to forge a private world of intimacy, independent of patriarchal gender divisions, founders as apartheid gains force, with Paul forced to recognize the irrelevance of his reformist activities to radicalized blacks.

The direction in which South Africa is moving is fully demonstrated when Helen witnesses the shooting of a black in a riot. Importantly, it is only when political violence impinges upon her that she recognizes the need to pursue her own life independent of the male. Helen's own presentation of the riot emphasizes her discovery of horror, as a fresh and real emotion: 'Everyone fears fear; but horror – that belongs to second-

20

hand experience, through books and films' (p. 325). This real experience, however, is swiftly trivialized by Paul as 'Helen's adventure at the barricades' (p. 327). Afterwards, she and her companion, Laurie, are invited together to gatherings, 'so that both might be present when the tale was told; and told it always was. Laurie developed quite a technique in the telling' (p. 327). Significantly, Helen is marginalized, her experience appropriated and narrated by the male. In frequent re-tellings, she comes to recognize the points at which Laurie, unvaryingly, pauses, drops his voice, or places his emphasis, until 'it was his technique only that I heard' (p. 328). As a result she feels 'as if I was never there at all'. Her real experience, unassimilable to secondhand concepts, has been emptied of content in favour of a male narrative. The episode thus makes two points. First it implicates the fashion in which men select and appropriate the significance of female experience, exercising male proxy over a woman's story. Second it exposes the emptiness of mere technique, suggesting the need for a form of narrative which can encompass the horror of black experience, without mediating it through ready-made conventions.

At the close of the novel, leaving Africa, Helen reassesses the form of her story: 'All this came back to me in shock and turbulence, not the way I have written it here, but in a thousand disconnected images' (p. 366). Simultaneously she recognizes discontinuity as the principle of her female existence, understanding that she had fled from the parental self-image in the belief that 'the real me was the one with Paul' (p. 348) only to discover that her earlier self was not so easily discounted: 'the person who lived with Paul only thought she was real' (p. 348). Rather than developing in a coherent fashion Helen has merely assumed different self-images. In consequence Helen now lays claim to her own story in order to emphasize its disjunctures and its episodic development:

> although no part of one's life can be said to come to an end except in death, nothing can be said to be a beginning but birth, life flows and checks itself, overlaps, flows again; and

21

it is in these pauses that a story is taken up, in these pauses that there comes the place at which it is inevitable to set it down. (p. 366)

Helen chooses to conclude her story, poised in limbo between Africa and Europe, as she observes a group of 'native minstrels' (p. 367) singing 'Paper Doll', an appropriate image of the arrested quality of both female and black development.

A WORLD OF STRANGERS

Where Helen's 'voyage in' ends in a voyage out of Africa, Gordimer's next novel, *A World of Strangers*, takes up almost where Helen left off, as Toby Hood docks at Mombasa, en route to Johannesburg and his British family's publishing business. Where *The Lying Days* almost ignores the black world to concentrate upon female development, *A World of Strangers* takes its narrator into the townships, particularly Sophiatown. Importantly Helen's internalized female world gives way here to cooler male narration, with inter-male relationships as the major focus. Gordimer described Sophiatown as 'a place of bachelors' whose casual relationships with women were 'rigidly excluded from the serious world of deep friendship between men'.[5] One such friendship develops between Toby and Steven Sitole, who are brought together by a shared desire to escape from the orthodoxy of Liberal opposition (Steven's non-participation in the Defiance Campaign, Toby's distaste for his parents' obsession with causes) into an apolitical private life (p. 96). The trio is completed by Toby's mistress, Cecil, temperamentally akin to Steven in her egocentric hedonism. The triangular relation occurs, however, in fractured form. Cecil and Steven never meet. Indeed, Toby deliberately conceals his friendship from prejudiced Cecil, in the knowledge that otherwise he would lose her. In his own person he therefore contributes to the maintenance of separate worlds. Primarily this separation results from the racial divisions of apartheid, as Toby oscillates between the High House, the Alexanders' luxurious mansion, and the House of Fame in Sophiatown. Additionally the erotic basis of Toby's motivation is worth noting; he refuses to sacrifice private sexual gratification, thus keeping his erotic world and the world of bachelors strictly apart. For Toby, women are themselves strangers 'another species than myself' (p. 77), their appeal dependent on 'remoteness' (p. 199) and 'exoticism' (p. 249). He jokes: 'I would choose an houri rather than a companion. No doubt what I had seen in the nasty woodshed of childhood was a serious-minded intellectual woman' (p. 249).

In the event Toby loses both Cecil and Steven, Cecil to a conventional marriage, Steven to death. Toby's desire to 'let the abstractions of race and politics go hang' (p. 34) founders upon the recognition that Steven's death, in a car-crash during a police chase, following a raid on an illicit shebeen, is a direct consequence of his colour. Toby is thus forced to recognize the deficiencies of a life lived in terms of personal realization, in a society where the large majority are legally prevented from pursuing any goals at all. The strength of his commitment remains, however, ambiguous. At the close, bidding farewell to Sam Mofokenzazi, Toby assures him that he will return to South Africa, but the pair are forced apart to descend their separate stairways, and Sam's last words, themselves ominous, are lost: 'Who knows with you people, Toby, man? Maybe you won't come back at all. Something will keep you away. Something will prevent you, and we won't—' (p. 254)

The limitations of Toby's personalism, which makes Cecil and Steven strangers to each other, are directly connected to his tendency to view South Africa in ironically detached terms, through a Eurocentric literary lens. Just as the whites exploit South Africa to gratify their personal desires (notably in the moneyed Alexanders' sporting philistinism) so Toby treats external reality purely as a means towards self-realization. Africa is thus mediated at secondhand, through ready-made concepts. The fashion in which Toby 'reads' Africa is clearly designed to warn the reader off any similar approach. Reader-

23

identification is also checked by Toby's ironic self-presentation, almost as a character-within-a-character. Thus, on arrival in Mombasa, he discards the facts of bluebooks and reports in favour of the exotic, casting himself successively as Sinbad (p. 18), a Dickens character (p. 10), and as an urban knight to Cecil's 'fair lady' (p. 104) of romance. Even his fellow passengers form a set of literary-colonial ghosts – the household advisor to an Indian prince, a Consul bound for the Congo, a woman who hails Mombasa as 'something out of Somerset Maugham' (p. 7). The latter's passion for Italy is described as Byronic, Forsterian (p. 14), introducing (in Clingman's succinct phrase) the 'generic debate with Forster'[6] which continues throughout the novel. When Toby arrives in Johannesburg it is only to discover that he has 'progressed merely from one unreality to another' (p. 35), as he takes up residence at the Stratford Hotel, its bar furnished with 'Tudor' chairs and a picture of Henry VIII. Michael Wade, who explores the recurrent theme of 'Europe in Africa' in Gordimer's fiction, characterizes the novel as 'a critique of the impact of the metropolitan culture, of its system of "meanings" or values, on South African society'.[7] In this context it is highly appropriate that Toby's purpose in Johannesburg is to promote books; he is too literary by half. In conversation at the High House he mistakes 'rider' for 'writer'. When a muddy, poorly executed Courbet is exhibited there, it draws admiring comments from guests who are automatically reverential to the values of metropolitan culture, and are themselves part of an artificially engineered 'English' society. (The Alexanders maintain a large and varied guestlist 'like publishers of paper-back novelettes': p. 133.)

Faced with the realization that 'Johannesburg seems to have no genre of its own' (p. 75) Toby is tempted to locate aesthetic and human vitality elsewhere, in Sophiatown. Although he scorns the convention, drawn from slice-of-life fiction, that its poverty makes it more 'real' (p. 149) he nevertheless admits that the township 'did for me what Italy or Greece had done for other Englishmen, in other times. It did not change me; it released me and made me more myself' (p. 154). Though Toby qualifies his views, the suspicion lingers that his identification of Steven with vital reality, reminiscent of Forster's Italians, stems from pre-inscribed assumptions. Nor are the black characters immune from the dominance of European cultural norms. Steven comments acerbically that Sam's jazz-opera, written in collaboration with a white, is

> more of a white man's idea of what a black man would write, and a black man's idea of what a white man would expect him to write, than the fusion of a black man's and a white man's worlds of imagination. (p. 201)

Yet as the artist of his life Steven draws himself in stereotyped terms, composing a 'picture of himself as the embittered, devil-may-care African' (p. 115). When he dies he is promptly converted into a cardboard martyr by the blacks: 'their sort of hero' (p. 245). Only one character, Anna Louw, a radical Afrikaner, sidesteps the delusions of this world. Importantly Anna's revolt began as a revolt of taste (p. 172) when she observed the disparity between her African surroundings and the simpering, touched-up photographs in her family home. The novel ends, however, with Anna imprisoned, reduced to a photograph in Toby's wallet. Gordimer's attack on the 'awful triumphant separateness' (p. 193) of apartheid, which makes all South Africans strangers to each other, is simultaneously a critique of the values of the Forsterian fictional paradigm, as connections break, friendships fail, and individual realization is dwarfed by political determinism.

The fragility of Toby's Eurocentric values becomes particularly apparent in the hunt in which he participates. In the veld the atavistic all-male group triumphs over Toby's bookish values. The books he brought remain unread (p. 228) as he re-enters a dated world of 'Edwardian' (p. 231) pleasures, reassuming the Imperial heritage rejected by his parents. Kitted out in hunting gear like 'props from an old Trader Horn film' (p. 213) Toby is now cast in the character of the white hunter. In the hunt Toby revels in a 'sudden, intense sense of my existence that is all I have ever known of a state of grace' (p. 226). Grace is also the name of the only feminine presence in the hunt, a setter bitch. After the hunt, Toby discovers her dead. He recalls the moment, when he learns of Steven's fate (p. 238). As the hunt is coterminous with Steven's death, pursued by other white hunters, it implicates the underlying violence of South African society, together with its retrogressive nature. The pursuit of indulgent self-realization is an anachronism, a grace now dead. Mere personal vitalism is insufficient. Where the setter bitch lives out a physical life to the end, when she simply drops, Steven is not granted even this level of existence, but is hunted down. Toby's desire to distance himself from the 'world of victims' (p. 30) of his parents is thus ironically fulfilled. Where internal exploration failed in *The Lying Days*, detachment and irony rebound upon the narrator of *A World of Strangers*. Arguably, the novel appears to be primarily diagnostic, contesting metropolitan values, but unable as yet to suggest a political or aesthetic remedy. It is only with Gordimer's third novel, *Occasion for Loving*, in which sexual and racial themes conjoin successfuly, that personalism is fully satirized in the subtextual psychoanalytics of the novel.

OCCASION FOR LOVING

In *Occasion for Loving*, Gordimer draws upon her childhood experience in order to transform a personal trauma into a political metaphor, to investigate the relation of love to power, and ultimately to reject the liberal tenets of her earlier fiction. Jessie Stilwell spends much of the novel renegotiating the terms of her existence by reassessing her past. Like Gordimer, the young Jessie was taken out of school aged 10 or 11, on the pretext of a nonexistent heart complaint, debarred from physical activity, and cocooned in a state of dependency by her unhappily married mother, as an emotional ally against the latter's European husband, Bruno Fuecht. Though Jessie appears to have put this lost adolescence behind her, as the novel opens she recognizes that in her subconscious 'she had never left her mother's house' (p. 9). Impelled by the catalyst of her awkward relationship with Morgan, her son by a previous marriage, Jessie undertakes a retrospective reconstruction of her past, a process which runs in tandem with her husband Tom's attempts to write an impartial history of Africa, which will present the African people as a historical subject in their own right, rather than as a subset of Eurocentric history.

Jessie's love-relationships are marked by a persistent oscillation between hothouse intimacy and emotional detachment. Struck by the potential symmetry between the triangular relationships of the young Jessie, her mother and stepfather, and Morgan, his mother and stepfather, she has deliberately attempted to avoid a repetition of the past, despatching Morgan to a distant school, and maintaining him at emotional arm's length. In contrast her vision of erotic love is romantic, individualist, and antisocial: 'to celebrate love, you must do no work, see no friends, ignore obligations' (p. 10). In her marriage Jessie is profoundly uneasy lest this romantic intimacy harden into a conventional relationship, conducted in the public eye in conformity with social norms: 'Like a dance that acts out some great ceremony whose meaning the dancers have forgotten' (p. 12). Her fear finds a political and aesthetic correlative when the Stilwells attend a mine-dancing. The adulterated tribal vaudeville of the dancers, performing a paid spectacle for tourists, has lost all connection with its original cultural content: 'It all meant nothing. . . . They mummed an ugly splendid savagery, a broken ethos, well lost; unspeakable sadness came to Jessie, her body trembled with pain. They sang and danced and trampled the past under their feet' (p. 37). The parallel with Jessie's own lost past, and with her fear that her own love relation with her partner will be ossified for public display, is reinforced when Jessie discovers that the neglected Morgan has been frequenting a taxi-dance joint. In her own youth Jessie could not dance; now Morgan has to seek out paid partners. Though Tom attempts to smooth glibly over the incident ('What was needed was an explanation, not the truth': p. 55) Jessie is forcibly reminded of the youth she missed. When she visits the dance hall, and is mistaken for a paid partner, the horrible possibility looms that despite her attempts to live and love on her own terms, the social conventions of bourgeois society will triumph in the future.

Up to this point Jessie had made most of her past inaccessible to her, in the psychological sense of the term. Now she realizes that in order to understand Morgan, she needs to grasp what she herself had been at his age. Her memories are presented as several sharply focused scenes. In one, she remembers awakening in the night to confront her mother outside the bathroom door, shaming the latter with her unspoken awareness that her mother has been making love with Fuecht. The incident, strongly suggestive of Freudian 'primal scene' content, highlights her ambivalence to her mother: 'was she trembling with pity and shame, for the outrage of her mother? . . . did she want, as well, to shame her mother' (p. 26). Though Mrs Fuecht loathes her husband, she remains married to him for his money, essentially performing the 'love-dance' (p. 190) as a paid partner. Another detail of Jessie's past surfaces with extraordinary vividness, a photograph of her dead father displayed between pictures of Jessie's favourite novelists. When her stepfather comes to her bedroom one night to restore the current to her lamp, he notices the photographs, assuming that they are screen-idols, 'great lovers' (p. 68). His error is percipient. In her sexual fantasies Jessie has made a lover out of her father's image, as the only young male face available to her projections. In a Freudian sense the photograph is a 'screen' image, obscuring the real focus of Jessie's erotic yearnings. At this point in the novel the reader assumes an ambivalent attraction to Fuecht on Jessie's part. In a subsequent memory Jessie remembers

The shape of cold terror that used to impress itself on the back of her neck when she turned her back to the dark passage behind the bathroom door. . . . Had she ever, in the twenty years or so since then, found out who it was that threatened to come up behind her? (p. 69)

28

The identification of Jessie's fear in Oedipal terms is strengthened by the juxtaposition of the two bathroom scenes, and by her remembered terror of brown electrical plugs, associated with Fuecht by his expertise with electricity, the meaning of his forename, Bruno, and by Jessie's sense of powerful emotional currents flowing 'electrically' (p. 70) through the household. The legitimacy of the amateur Freudian reading is called into question, however, by Tom's meeting with Fuecht, in the present, which interrupts the sequence of memories. Like Jessie, Tom thinks he knows the facts of his wife's past, aware that though Jessie had felt dependent upon her mother, in reality her mother, starved of love, was 'passionately and ruthlessly dependent upon her' (p. 76). What Tom now discovers is that Fuecht did in fact father Jessie, by an adulterous affair. Significantly Tom, the impartial historian, never tells Jessie. The sham of Tom's respect for truth is thus revealed simultaneously with the bogusness of Jessie's assumptions about the past, and the inefficacy of her quest for individual integration through a past conceived, erroneously, in terms of a Eurocentric psychological fiction. The positioning of her father's photograph between novelists is therefore singularly appropriate; he is himself only a convenient fiction.

A second catalyst in Jessie's self-exploration is provided by the presence in her household of Ann and Boaz Davis. At the end of Part One of the novel, Jessie suddenly discovers that, while she has been plumbing her past, Ann Davis has launched herself into an affair with Gideon Shibalo, a black painter. A brilliant dancer (p. 93), Ann is increasingly drawn to Gideon through an attraction described as having 'the rhythm of a dance' (p. 104). Living unreflectingly in the present she provides an alter ego to Jessie, an image of that younger self who might have been. Although Jessie values the intimate privacy of her marriage, she tolerates her house-guests on good liberated grounds: 'You've got to get away from the tight little bourgeois family unit' (p. 243). She extends a similar tolerance to the interracial affair, confident that for her 'the race business' (p. 253) had been settled long ago. In the triangle of Boaz–

Ann–Gideon, however, she comes to see that this is not the case. As she tells Gideon, 'It's the truth, the rational truth, that a love affair like yours is the same as any other. But you haven't come to the truth while it's still only the rational truth' (p. 253). The love affair provides its own parallels to the impasse which Jessie feels between intimacy and detachment. Gideon remarks on the hothouse quality of interracial relationships: 'Every contact with whites was touched with intimacy; for even the most casual belonged by definition to the conspiracy against keeping apart. It was always easier . . . to have a love-affair than a friendship' (p. 120). Like Jessie, Ann begins the novel in a state of apparent colour-blindness. On the road with Gideon, however, forced to assume the role of white 'madam' travelling with her 'boy', Ann discovers a fatal ease of adaptation to the dominant cultural conventions, 'fitting an identity imposed from outside herself' (p. 238). She becomes aware of Gideon as a black first, as a man second. As Stephen Clingman has observed, the affair fails, not because of state intervention (the 1950 Immorality Act) but from within: 'no external sanctions are needed to break up the relationship between Ann and Gideon because the repressions of apartheid have become psychologically inscribed. In this regard it is the prestructuring effects of apartheid that count.'[8] Initially Jessie's own prestructuring appears to be Oedipal. Ironically when she retreats to a beachhouse, leaving Morgan behind, she finds herself beset not by her son's emotional demands but by Ann and Gideon who descend upon her. As a result she discovers the prestructuring effects of apartheid upon her own psyche. In conversation with Gideon she suddenly recognizes her childhood fear as emanating from

> The black man that I must never be left alone with in the house. . . . I used to feel, at night, when I turned my back to the dark passage . . . that someone was coming up behind me. Who was it, do you think? And how many more little white girls are there for whom the very first man was a black man? The very first man, the man of the sex phantasies. (p. 253)

Jessie's earlier memories are thus placed as screen memories, obscuring a culturally inscribed fear behind a Eurocentic psychological fiction. At the close of the novel she comes to understand that the source of her repressions, the central taboo, is not the European father, but the black African. Jessie has been constructed by an African past; her admission historicizes her trauma, now comprehensible not as the individualist product of bourgeois repressions within the nuclear family, but as stemming from political and social conditions. The novel therefore turns away from the illegitimate timelessness of the Freudian fiction, to historicize desire, and to impel a realization of the relation of love to power.

A series of parallels between Jessie and Gideon substantiates Jessie's awareness that 'love – even sex – is nearly always power instead' (p. 154). Jessie's mother used her power, together with the fictional heart complaint, to interrupt Jessie's schooling and to perpetuate a relationship of dependency. The South African state withdraws Gideon's passport, preventing him from taking up a scholarship to study art abroad. As a black man Gideon's past has been annulled by Eurocentric historians; Jessie's by the collusion of her historian husband and European father. Jessie's apparent dependence on her mother, in reality dependent upon her, provides a precise parallel with the systematic South African underdevelopment of blacks, maintained in dependency and treated as children by whites who depend upon their labour.[9] In the context of institutional repression, there can be no occasion for loving between white and black. Gordimer, herself, has commented on the failure of South African Liberalism, in the context of her own realization that 'apparently transcendental private relationships are in fact pretty meaningless, trapped in political determinism'.[10] The Stilwells are similarly confronted with the inefficacy of their liberal, humanist creed. The moral is drawn directly:

They believed in the integrity of personal relations against the distortions of law and society. What stronger and more proudly personal bond was there than love? Yet even

31

between lovers they had seen blackness count, the personal return inevitably to the social, the private to the political. . . . So long as the law remained unchanged, nothing could bring integrity to personal relationships. (p. 279)

Jessie is none the less slow to absorb the lesson. In the final scene Jessie approaches Gideon affectionately, only to be told, 'White bitch – get away' (p. 288). The price of her awareness of his blackness is the recognition of her whiteness; she is as much a type to Gideon as is the black man to her fantasy projections. Though Gideon, drunk, forgets the exchange, amnesia is at an end for Jessie, now restored to historical consciousness: 'So long as Gideon did not remember, Jessie could not forget' (p. 288).

If *Occasion for Loving* calls into question the traditional themes and values of the Liberal novel with its Forsterian watchword, 'Only connect', and its apolitical emphasis upon the primacy of personal relationships in opposition to the facts of cultural and social difference, it also upsets fictive conventions. The deconstruction of the Eurocentric psychological fiction is accompanied by a subtle subversion of narrative expectations. Quite overtly the luxury of the concept of rounded character is exposed. Jessie's personal quest for identity, negotiated vicariously through a series of shadow selves, past and present (Ann, Gideon, Morgan), culminates not in integration into wholeness but in the realization that she is a 'flat' character, a type. Gordimer has recalled that a black South African had challenged her view that the presentation of white characters by black novelists was limited by caricature. On the contrary, he asserted, 'this is the way most whites *are* as far as most blacks are concerned; it is the whole truth about whites for most blacks'.[11] Jessie's attempts to forge connections with her past self founder upon the discontinuities of her divided society. She can only connect with Gideon either on a level of fantasy, or in terms of their public identities. Psychic integration is mocked by legally enforced segregation. Other connections are also shortcircuited. No explanation is provided for Ann's sudden departure with Boaz. The Stilwells, in common with the reader, are left in a similar position to the madwoman whom Jessie observes 'sewing without any thread in the needle. It flashed in and out of the stuff, empty, connecting nothing with nothing' (p. 44).

The discontinuities of personal experience in a fractured society are also those of art. If the withdrawal of his scholarship cuts Gideon off from European traditions, he is equally isolated from the tribal traditions which Boaz, a musicologist, memorializes. The latter are themselves dying out, extinguished with their craftsmen, the musical instruments now constructed from urban materials. Gordimer's ambivalent awareness of the need to adapt the novel to African conditions, to avoid exercising a white proxy in the arts, emerges in the treatment of Ann and Jessie, as surrogate artists. Ann, who can play any instrument, sing along to any melodic pattern (p. 150), eventually reveals a facile adaptability to dominant cultural conventions. In contrast, Ann observes Jessie as the conductor of her family's emotional life, recognizing in a family row 'the tiny motif' of a forgotten incident 'now fully orchestrated' (p. 91) by Jessie. Gordimer has stated[12] her approval of Lukács's condemnation of the modernist novel, with its subjectivism, obsession with pathological states and ahistorical presentation of the human condition. Jessie, locked in subjective, ahistorical, psychological enquiry, romances her life in a fashion which evades its horrors. A ghastly family Christmas, for example, is converted by Jessie into a comic story, which in subsequent retellings becomes familiar, and thus defused, 'an explosive from which the detonator had long been removed' (p. 45). Gordimer's own oblique approach to the affair between Gideon and Ann, presented almost at a tangent to Jessie's story, is a strategy which succeeds in avoiding its conversion into the clichés of the South African novel of miscegenation, while leaving its explosive force still primed. As the vicarious observer of the affair Jessie occupies a position akin to that of a reader. At the beach her own experience of reading implicitly constructs an alternative reader for

Gordimer's own fiction. There Jessie discovers that *The Magic Mountain* is not an old-fashioned novel of 'character and furniture but a terrifying descent through the "safety" of middle-class trappings to the individual anarchy and ideological collapse lying at their centre' (p. 198). When Ann and Gideon appear, at this point, to interrupt Jessie's reading, the parallel with Gordimer's own fiction is apparent. The quotation becomes proleptic of the next phase of Gordimer's development, in which bougeois conventions come under attack, and the problematic necessity of a historicized aesthetic is fully explored.

2

THE REVOLUTION THAT FAILED

Gordimer's two subsequent novels, both profoundly influenced by Marxist thinkers, reflect her evolution away from liberal meliorism. Both may be read as fictions of a revolution which failed, *The Late Bourgeois World* chronicling the unsuccessful activities of a naive white revolutionary, against the background of the crushing of South African opposition in the 1960s, *A Guest of Honour* moving out to examine the theme in broader terms, in a hypothetical African state. Both pair male and female protagonists, the one beginning on the death of Max Van Den Sandt, who is remembered by his ex-wife Liz over the course of one day, the other concluding with the death of the male, leaving the heroine to continue into the future. Quite overtly, each novel moves towards a more committed social aesthetic, with *The Late Bourgeois World* forming something of an aesthetic manifesto.

In *The Late Bourgeois World* Liz Van Den Sandt ponders: 'what could one say this is the age of?' (p. 113). Her lover, Graham, responds : 'I've just read a book that refers to ours as the Late Bourgois World' (p. 114). The work in question, Ernst Fisher's *The Necessity of Art*[13], forms a vital intertext to the novel. In her 1985 Tanner lectures[14] Gordimer referred approvingly to Fisher, a Marxist critic, when arguing that art represents the freedom of the spirit and is therefore automatically on the side of the oppressed. Essentially Fisher sets out to investigate 'the necessity of art – as well as its questionable role in the late bourgeois world' (Fisher, p. 17). For Fisher all art is conditioned by time and represents humanity as it corresponds to the ideas and aspirations of a particular historical situation. Locating the origins of art in its utility he argues that 'art in the dawn of humanity had little to do with "beauty" and nothing at all to do with any aesthetic desire: it was a magic tool or weapon of the human collective in its struggle for survival' (Fisher, pp. 35–6). Thereafter, in his argument, art evolved towards a transformative social function, enlightening men in societies grown opaque. Fisher thus envisages socialist art as a means of going beyond contemporary isolation, reuniting the individual with communal existence. In this analysis, late bourgois art fails because it lacks a vision of the future, as opposed to the hopeful historical perspective of socialist art: 'In a decaying society art . . . must also reflect decay. . . . Art must show the world as changeable. And help to change it' (Fisher, p. 48). Liz's unemotional objectivity and deadpan tone, adversely commented upon by critics, register as pathological symptoms of the decaying, dehumanized world which she inhabits. If *The Late Bourgeois World* is none the less Liz's story, rather than Max's, it is so as a result of an eventual recognition of the historical condition as transformative.

Importantly Liz's conversation with Graham occurs against the backdrop of one of a series of super-sunsets, 'a romanticised picture that made the room look drab' (p. 109). For Liz, the sunset, possibly the result of nuclear fallout, cannot be beautiful. When Graham contends that 'There's nothing moral about beauty' (p. 109) Liz's rejoinder 'Truth is *not* beauty' (p. 110) crisply foregrounds the question of the moral basis of art and, by extension in the Keatsian echo, that of the relation of art to time. In Fisher's analysis the late bourgeois world has become so complex as to create a desire to simplify reality, and to present human beings as linked by elementary rather than material relations, a process culminating in the triumph of myth in art: 'Mystification and myth-making in the late bourgeois world offer a way of evading social decisions'

(Fisher, p. 95). In consequence myth opposes an ahistorical 'essential' man to man as he develops in society, falsifying the specific nature of a historical moment into a general idea of 'being', presenting a socially conditioned world as cosmically unconditional, and transforming man into a hieroglyph in a play of transcendent mysteries. Where Graham envisages the sunset in aestheticist terms, supplying a Chagallian image of floating lovers (p. 109) which encapsulates the mystic desire for flight from reality, Liz finds it curiously dated: 'Like the background to a huge Victorian landscape. Something with a quotation underneath with lots of references to the Soul and God's Glory and the Infinite . . . what my grandmother would have been taught was beautiful' (p. 110). Thus the overblown sunset suggests to Liz only the absurdity of an atemporal, transcendent aesthetic, an understanding which derives from her preceding visit to her grandmother on the latter's 87th birthday.

Earlier, Liz had contrasted the unchanging landscape of the veld with her awareness, fostered by Max's death, that 'Time is change' (p. 12). Reassessing Max's radical activities she recognizes that, though his life was an apparent failure (ineffectual sabotage, gaol, betrayal of associates, suicide) he was at least intent upon change, motivated by a desire for community with blacks in reaction against the atomized individualism of his bourgeois background. Even in death Max remains more alive to Liz than the inhabitants of the claustral world of South Africa. In the home for the aged, where 'There was no sense of the day of the week. . . . No seasons either. Spring or winter it feels the same' (p. 95), her grandmother's senile amnesia projects a nightmarish image of timeless stasis. Imagistically the two women are associated when Graham sends them identically funereal bouquets. When, in sudden terror of death, the old lady asks 'What happened?', the answer is suggested by the decor of her room (signed photographs of the artists of her youth) in which 'it always seems that nothing has happened' (p. 98). In the great nullity of her existence, living upon dividends from past capital, the old lady, emblematic of the South

African bourgeoisie, will know change only as death. When she cross-questions Liz anxiously on the topic of current fashion ('What are they wearing this year? Will it be black?') Liz's response (white 'but not *dead* white': p. 103) implies her recognition of the need to move beyond a bourgeois world which has become a living death.

A means of escape from this becalmed Limbo is offered by Luke Fokase, who asks Liz to use her power of attorney over her grandmother's bank-account to channel funds to the PAC. Liz recognizes Luke as 'my Orpheus', come to fetch 'pale Eurydice' from her 'life-insured Shades' (p. 150). As Abdul R. JanMohamed has suggested,[15] Gordimer ironizes a myth, transforming Luke, a member of the political underworld, into Liz's rescuer from the terminal white laager. The particular mythic reference carries both an aesthetic and a political message. Gordimer's implicit riposte to those critics who regard the activity of the novelist as irrelevant to political events recalls Sartre's 'Orphée Noir',[16] the essay which marked the first attempt to come to terms with negritude, as both a historical and an aesthetic force, revalorizing African myths to radical ends.

At the close of the novel Max's death has been superseded as news by the technological exploits of man in space. Fisher described art in the late bourgeois world as in danger of being 'driven out by science and technology. When the human race can fly to the moon is there any real need for moonstruck poets? . . . The astronaut can see what the poet merely dreamed of' (Fisher, p. 217). In the final sequence, drifting in and out of sleep, Liz is initially attracted by the images of the astronauts as expressing 'the same old yearning for immortality, akin to all our desires to transcend all kinds of human limits' (p. 154). She comes back to earth with a bump, however, as her thoughts move to Luke's suggestion. In the existence of the bank account, a means of turning the weapons of South African capitalism against itself, Liz finds an alternative answer to her grandmother's question: 'The bank account is there. It can probably be used for this purpose. What happened, the old lady asked me. Well, that's what's happened' (p. 159). Though Gordimer leaves Liz's future decision open, the novel closes on a note which suggests that this Eurydice will follow her Orpheus into the future without looking back. Though lying in timeless darkness, Liz finds that her heart supplies the temporal beat: 'There is no clock in the room . . . but the slow even beats of my heart repeat to me, like a clock: afraid, alive, afraid, alive, afraid, alive . . .' (p. 160). Human time eclipses the mystificatory attractions of technological transcendence. Though Liz's foetal position associates her with the astronaut ('a dim foetal creature attached by a sort of umbilical cord to a dim vehicle': p. 107) it also suggests the possibility of rebirth into a world of historical rather than metaphysical meaning. In Liz's mind, the thought of the bank account grows 'like sexual tumescence' (p. 146) an image which indicates the reawakening of Liz's deadened emotions, and anticipates the central concerns of the novel which follows.

A GUEST OF HONOUR

In interview Gordimer said of *A Guest of Honour*, 'I tried to write a political novel treating the political theme as personally as a love story',[17] a comment which suggests a marked change in direction after the anaesthetized coolness of *The Late Bourgeois World*. As in the preceding novel, two stories are interwoven, that of Bray, a Liberal white returning to an unnamed, newly independent African country, and that of his lover Rebecca, whose story continues after Bray's death. For most critics, Bray's is the story of the novel. Rebecca's tends to be scanted as lacking clear relation to political events. The novel therefore immediately provokes questions. Whose story is it? That of a newly liberated colony sinking back into neo-colonialism and authoritarian structures? That of a Liberal individual, Bray, torn between personal and collective demands? Or that of a love-relationship, to which the minutely observed sociopolitical detail is only a backdrop? In deliberately fostering this uncertainty of focus between collective, individual, and relational stories, Gordimer sets out to interrogate the connections between the political and the sexual. Writing in 1970, a year which saw Kate Millett's *Sexual Politics* and Shulamith Firestone's *The Dialectic of Sex*, both works which examine the psychopathology of power, Gordimer constructs a double plot designed to explore the interaction of the ideological and the psychological. The sexual relationship between Bray and Rebecca therefore lies at the centre of a novel which investigates the psychological causes of authoritarianism and of failed revolutions, deriving its conceptual framework from Wilhelm Reich's psychoanalytic hypothesis, and from an informed awareness of psycholinguistic theory.

In *A Guest of Honour* Hjalmar Wentz, prompted by a recent biography of Reich, remembers that in his youth in Germany Reich had been a hero: 'But while we were discussing the sexual revolution as the break with authoritarianism in the father-dominated family, others were already kissing the feet of Father Hitler' (p. 418). In response Bray speculates: 'what would Reich have thought of the authoritarianism of this continent now – the sexual basis of authoritarianism according to his theory simply doesn't exist in African societies' (p. 418). Reich, whose ideas sprang back into prominence in the 'liberated' Sixties, is generally identified as the first Freudo-Marxist to relate the ideological to the psychological process. Where Freud held that society is founded upon repression and that nature and culture are always in opposition, Reich argued that instinct is good until adulterated by repressions, and that freedom from repression would lead to social progress. Thus where Freud is the economist of the sexual life, his therapy aimed at better management of the instincts, Reich is its Karl Marx, using psychoanalysis for revolutionary purposes, maintaining that by liberating the instincts one could create the condition for an irrevocable liberation of man in society. Reich's analysis of the failure of the Russian revolution (*The Mass Psychology of Fascism*) is particularly relevant to *A Guest of Honour*. For Reich all political revolutions, whether

40

of the Right or the Left, will fail if they are only political and economic, and do not extend to the repressive morality of everyday life. In contrast to orthodox Marxists Reich envisages man as instinctual and therefore insists upon the supreme role played by irrationality as opposed to class or economic interests in history. In an intuition akin to Gramsci's concept of hegemony, Reich contends that the oppression of the masses by the ruling classes is inexplicable merely in terms of the material power wielded by the latter. Rather the ruling classes are successful in controlling the masses because bourgeois society creates people with a character structure which renders them submissive to authority and willing to be ruled. In his argument repression is the result of the establishment of authoritarian patriarchy, with the family envisaged as the factory in which the state's structure and ideology are moulded. The inhibition of sexuality thus renders the child docile, obedient and fearful of authority. In consequence, revolutions fail because rebels see authority figures, unconsciously, as their own childhood fathers. However radical the revolution, so long as the family persists, authority creeps back. Rebellions of sons against fathers therefore permit the return of the father in the character of the son. In Philip Rieff's succinct comment:

> Habits of domestic living are concrete ways in which ideology internalises authority. Unless a revolution conquers the bedroom it cannot conquer; without a rearrangement of intimacy, men will continue to identify themselves, if not with old rulers, then with old rules of conduct.[18]

Interestingly Reich understood liberalism as functioning in society much as the superego operates in the psyche, as a sham of civility laid over the reality of conflict, and therefore powerless against doctrines of conflict once they break through the surface of social life. In Reich's account patriarchal society also demands that the child distinguish between love and sex, with sexual desire considered as an inappropriate response to the mother.

Reich's ideas offer important points of contact with *A Guest of Honour*, in which national liberation reverts to authoritarianism (the British army is invited back by a dictatorial President to suppress revolt), in which one major protagonist, Bray, is a Liberal whose creed proves insufficient to the demands of a period of dynamic social conflict, and in which the other major protagonist, Rebecca, both promiscuous and a mother, confronts the problematic separation of sex and love. Bray himself has to choose between his wife, Olivia, and his mistress, apparently a choice between love and sex, and between Mweta, the President for whom he feels considerable affection, and the less likeable Shinza, who encapsulates radical power. Mweta and Olivia are continually associated in Bray's mind, through plot parallels and via a series of letters exchanged concurrently with both, but are eventually abandoned in favour of Rebecca and Shinza, with the sexual relationship evolving in tandem with a growing political commitment. The basic political alternatives facing the new state are outlined by Shinza, quoting Julius Nyerere's Arusha declaration (1967): 'We have made a mistake to choose money. . . . The development of a country is brought about by people, not by money' (p. 362). Mweta's eventual choice of economic gradualism supported by foreign investment, as opposed to Shinza's brand of African socialism (popular participation, immediate improvement of the condition of the masses) is aligned with the choice of money rather than of people, a choice reproduced at the personal level by the psychological structures of western capitalism.

At first the novel appears to bear out Bray's contention that the sexual basis of authoritarianism is lacking in an African context. Though Mweta is the 'father of the state' (p. 15), he is young, feminine in appearance, and actively determined to introduce a democratic social system 'in place of a paternalist discipline' (p. 17). In the opening pages of the novel, the authoritarian or phallic male is conspicuous only by his absence. 'Poor old' (p. 15) Shinza, 'Poor old' (p. 15) Roly Dando, the Attorney General, 'Old Hjalmar' (p. 16) and Boxer, another quasi-bachelor, complete the group of older males

42

who have 'drifted the moorings of family ties' (p. 114). Bray himself swiftly reverts to bachelor habits, keeping house with his old manservant, Kalimo. Indeed, even his masculine identity is attenuated. Described at one point as one of the 'fairy-godmothers' (p. 27) at the christening of the new state, he shares one forename with Evelyn Odara, a woman, and his attempts to remain politically neutral are repeatedly associated with being 'old-maidishly composed' (p. 68), 'hennish' (p. 197), and 'virginal' (p. 214). In the background the impression of sexual ambivalence is reinforced by the image of the White Fathers, 'shy as young girls' (p. 77) in their robes, the male Gala nanny, and the jokes about the lack of physical charms of Aleke's secretary, also male. The old, the desexualized and the child predominate. It surprises Bray that a rural school-teacher's pupil is his wife and a mother of four. Even Rebecca, also a mother, makes her entrance as 'a big, untidy schoolgirl' (p. 26), later to reappear with a 'good chap' (p. 109) smile as Aleke's secretary. The opening therefore implicitly poses questions. Will the children of the emancipated state evolve towards a new freedom, unconstrained by familial or sexual restraints? Or will political liberation be perceived as desexualization and emasculation, with predictable authoritarian results?

The permanence and durability of patriarchal structures are indicated in the family groups presented for the reader's inspection. Observing Mweta's large brood, Bray wonders how he will cope as President with the demands of the African extended family, only to learn that Mweta is employing a white housekeeper who banishes the children from the parental table. Areas of the mansion are to be walled off from outsiders, with the children relegated to a 'jungle gym' (p. 60) in the garden. Where Mweta appears to be moving away from relaxed African structures, Aleke has visibly never abandoned authoritarianism. A father of seven, he is entirely dictatorial towards his wife, in whose presence he behaves as if she were invisible. If the resistance of the authoritarian father to any weakening of his power is indicated in these westernized and indigenous African families, the fate of Hjalmar Wentz strikes a more ominous note. A Liberal who saved his Jewish wife, Margo, from Nazi Germany, Hjalmar has brought up his children in consciously libertarian fashion. But in his daughter history repeats itself. Emmanuelle imitates her father's previous action, smuggling her lover, Ras Asahe, out of the country. Ras, however, is implicated in a right-wing coup. When Emmanuelle flees, Margo turns on Hjalmar: 'A Jewish father would have had some authority over his daughter' (p. 419). Importantly the evolution of Hjalmar's family from enlightened Liberalism to the demand for an authoritarian father finds its parallel in political events. Mweta's authority has been challenged by the coup, which was whipped up on the accusation that he lacked 'the strong arm' (p. 422) to hold down Shinza and the unions. The political history of the state is itself marked by a conflict between fathers and sons. Mweta describes Shinza, his former mentor, as 'my father' (p. 162). As events develop, however, Mweta evolves from son back to father, replicating the authoritarian structures which he originally sought to destroy, instituting a preventive detention act by Hitlerian midnight broadcast, and arming the Company guards. The conjunction of Margo's wrath with Mweta's show of muscle, each the result of a right-wing coup, underlines the consonance of familial and political structures.

In the intervening period, the initial sexual equality of the new state also founders. Women are excluded from the Party Congress. One scene, an expensive banquet, foreshadows future events. While the chairman of mining companies adopts a 'patriarchal' (p. 193) tone, the sexes separate, the black men drawn to the male cameraderie of business talk, the white men exchanging obscene anecdotes, the white women giggling like schoolgirls, the black women patiently enduring neglect. Doris Manyema's mission to the UN does not protect her from the ogling advances of a furtive white male, mesmerized by her breasts. The evening culminates in a tableau in which Joy and Adamson Mweta sing together, Joy's 'motherly body in its schoolgirlish pink dress' (p. 196) an appropriate image of repression-as-innocence, Mweta recast in the acceptable role of black entertainer. The entire scene demonstrates the triumph of repression in relation to neo-colonialist paternalism, from the fake asexuality of the Mwetas, to the obscene innuendos which surround them. Just as the political lines are hardening, so the sexual lines have not been redrawn.

What, however, of Bray's individual involvement in these events? His love affair does not appear to be politically radical in its consequences. Sexual permissiveness in no way threatens bourgeois property values. Indeed Bray takes active steps to safeguard Rebecca's property (significantly the proceeds of the sale of a house, *her* father's gift) smuggling her capital out to Switzerland. This compromising act highlights the ambiguity of the choice between people or money. In choosing Rebecca, Bray acts on personal motives, yet in consequence bleeds settler capital from an impoverished country. Superficially it might appear that Bray has simply reverted to older cultural patterns, betraying his wife and his Liberal conscience in favour of immediate sexual gratification with a younger female. Jean Fido[19] reads the novel in these terms, as the tale of a paternal colonialist, relinquishing political power, and therefore reasserting it on sexual grounds. Similarly Shinza's original choice of people yields swiftly to the need for hard cash with which to buy arms. When Bray is murdered he is en route for Europe, partly to take Rebecca to safety, partly to seek funds for Shinza. Though the murder is a mistake (Bray has been misidentified as a white mercenary) the suspicion lingers that he is, in a sense, a mercenary in Shinza's employ. Similar ambiguities surround Rebecca's fate. Though Rebecca evolves from mother to lover, despatching her children to South Africa of all places, she remains in Gala both for love of Bray and out of financial necessity. She finally departs in the company of Loulou Kamboya, a currency smuggler who travels with his own prostitutes. One of the latter, buttressed around with banknotes, is brought along 'more as a piggybank than une petite folie' (p. 485). The potential identification of Rebecca's liberated sexuality with mere whoredom is reinforced when she is repeatedly accosted by soldiers looking for prostitutes (p. 487) and when she receives her cash in Switzerland: 'She was like Loulou's girl, now, with a variety of currencies about her' (p. 494).

Rebecca is rewarded for her affair with her father's money, gained on production of a password, *La Fille Aux Yeux D'Or*, which conjoins erotic and economic concerns. Though Bray selects the codeword in tribute to Rebecca's eyes, Balzac's novel, in which the eponymous heroine is sold into prostitution, opens with an infernal evocation of the cupidity of Paris, its denizens in pursuit only of 'Gold or pleasure', in a world in which there are 'no true kinsmen but the thousand franc note',[20] an appropriate image of a society in which money triumphs over people. At the close of the novel Bray is also written off in a literary reference as Mweta's 'White Man Friday'. Potentially, therefore, both protagonists' stories may be read as a regression to older patterns of behaviour, in Bray's case to patriarchal, colonialist norms, in Rebecca's to her earlier promiscuity, now exacerbated and rewarded. The reader is left to ponder a series of questions. Does Rebecca remain in Gala for Bray or for her money? Is her story only a tale of erotic and economic exploitation? Does Bray leave Africa as Shinza's agent, or as Rebecca's lover? Is he a hapless victim or a mercenary? Is he liberated, in a radical sense, discovering with Rebecca an essential self beyond his liberal repressions, or is he the dupe of a patriarchal, phallic model of identity?

The answers to these questions, powerfully posed by Gordimer, must be sought in a second major concern of the novel, that of its own adequacy to the articulation of African realities. As the literary references above imply, Gordimer is aware of a potential mismatch between western literary norms and her particular subject. From the outset of the novel Bray is situated in a world marked by selective story-telling, and a struggle for interpretive control of events. At the Independence celebrations each character produces his own 'Independence story' and the air teems with anecdotes. Bray's acceptance by the group is explicitly envisaged in terms which compare linguistic norms with cultural and familial assumptions. He finds it 'rather like being forced to learn a foreign language by finding oneself alone among people who spoke nothing else: it was assumed that he would pick up family and other relationships merely by being exposed to them' (p. 23). Gordimer's interrogation of the relation between ideology and psychology finds literary extension in psycholinguistic terms. In an essay[21] Gordimer referred to the word as 'the primary homeland', replacing cultural loyalties for the writer. The phrase was drawn from George Steiner's discussion of man as 'the language animal', conditioned by language in every significant respect. Drawing on Whorf and Lacan, Steiner argues that patterns of thought echo the systematizations of language, which carries culturally ordained values. Thus the western sense of time as sequential causality, and of the irreducible status of the individual, is inseparable from patterns of Indo-European syntax, with its past, present and future tenses, and pronomial distinction between ego and collectivity. As Steiner comments, 'To learn a language beside one's native idiom, to penetrate its syntax, is to open for oneself a second window on the landscape of being.'[22] The consequences for psychology of this line of reasoning are drastic. Given that psychology is topographic, a piece of local inventory mapping the mental conventions of a specific culture (e.g. Freud's Vienna) then where consciousness communicates in a different linguistic context, a different psychology may be in order. Lacan's attempt to refound Freud's theory of psychic processes on a linguistic basis has established that psychology cannot be separated from an awareness of how radically a particular language conditions the life of the mind. In Steiner's argument, this selectivity of language is nowhere more evident than in literature. Every work of literature is a specialized language act, a piece of language in a heightened condition of order, reference, and elision, a selection filtering out some material from the available totality. In *A Guest of Honour* Gordimer draws attention to this process of omission, so that, at the close, as Bray's life story is submerged in a wash of journalistic mendacity, the reader is alerted to the possibility of absent stories, and of silences in the text.

One such story concerns Rebecca. When Bray first notices Rebecca in Gala he comments that 'there was some story there nobody bothered to ask' (p. 133). In his first sexual encounter with her the emphasis on desire and silence has been read (e.g. Fido) as indicative of Bray's regressive sexuality, satisfying male lust on an anonymous female. Alternatively (to draw on Michel Foucault's insights) it may indicate a recognition on Gordimer's part that to bring sexuality into the clear light of language is only to succeed in further controlling and repressing it. The need to rescue sexuality from secrecy and repression involves the simultaneous recognition that the recreation of sexuality in language must also resist language. In later sexual encounters Bray recognizes that 'words were reunited with the sweet mucous membrane from which they had been torn' (p. 279).

On this first occasion, the political theme is also emphasized. Making love, Bray is obsessed with thoughts of Shinza. Immediately beforehand Bray had visited Shinza discovering that, far from being an old has-been, Shinza has fathered a son on a new young wife. The memory of the boy haunts Bray who identifies Shinza in phallic terms as having 'another kind of confidence . . . not just in the mind, but in the body, in the senses' (p. 129). Reflecting on Shinza, Bray's incipient erection collapses when 'his mind switched to Mweta again, and his body shrank' (p. 130). Yet Bray's apparent defection to Shinza as phallic father is not quite as simple as it appears. Another 'boy' is discovered at Shinza's and a different story emerges. On the road Bray had picked up a taciturn hitchhiker, unresponsive to his polite 'interrogation' (p. 110). Shinza reveals that the youth has been in illegal detention for the entire period of Bray's sojourn in Gala, a fact well-known to authoritarian Aleke, though Bray 'never heard a word' (p. 121). Mweta has learnt how to 'shut people up', both verbally and physically. When Bray insists on eliciting the details, Shinza responds as if 'explaining to a child, "James, his head wouldn't answer, so they put their questions on his back"' (p. 124). The implicit parallel between physical and linguistic repression reveals to Bray that for Mweta 'words are whips, blows, and weapons, taken on the body and given on the bodies of others' (p. 169). Though Bray intervenes to have the responsible party (Lebaliso) removed, he realizes that there would continue to be other such incidents 'about which nobody would hear' (p. 139). The event thus looks forward proleptically to Bray's own death, an incident which is also misread and silenced at the close of the novel. The boy's torture is 'an old story' (p. 127), just as Bray's affair with Rebecca is an old story. But the juxtaposition of the two stories which 'nobody bothered to ask' suggests that Bray is not one to silence others, sexually or politically, and that he is not drawn to Shinza purely as an embodiment of male power, but as a figure intent on protecting the boy and others like him from the abuses of such power.

After the discovery of the detainee's story Bray increasingly finds that his own language is no longer adequate to his needs. The point is developed through a series of evasive letters exchanged with Mweta and Olivia, which offer in their measured arguments and impersonal tone a glaring contrast to the omissions and silences of their author. One such letter, from Olivia, extolling the joys of impersonal love for a grand-child, prompts the recognition that 'There was a growing gap between his feelings and his actions, and in that gap . . . the meaning lay' (p. 244). Eventually Bray's silences in his letters reduce his expression to automatic writing, 'something he picked up with a pen. It functioned of itself' (p. 269). The irrelevance of the letters (and by extension of polite letters, of literature) to Bray's African experience is underscored when Bray meets a rural schoolteacher, whose examination paper, imbued with the assumptions of colonial culture, invites the examinee to write a letter describing a school tour of the Continent, or a visit to a picture gallery. Bray writes just such a letter to Olivia after the Party Congress, relieved to have some 'objectively interesting' (p. 374) material, suitable for public consumption by Olivia's family.

Importantly the Congress also centres upon the opposition between formal discourse and a powerful silence. Beneath the jargon of the delegates, the strings of quotations and statistics, runs a silent subtext – the struggle for power between Mweta and Shinza. For Bray, Shinza has always been a speaking presence, not to be subsumed in the language of others: 'There are people in whom one reads signs, and others, on the surface equally typical, whose lives do not speak' (p. 319). At the Congress, however, it is Mweta who does not speak, winning the vital vote on a tactic of silence. The irrationality of political action is insisted upon as delegates ignore Shinza's ideological arguments to vote for the authority of Mweta's silence, which capitalizes on their subconscious needs.

Gordimer's novel also refuses to maintain the text at the level of formal discourse or public statement. The sense of a developing story in which Bray is a participant rather than a controlling observer emerges strongly in events in Gala. As one scene demonstrates, the redefinition of psyche and of language are interdependent. Bray has been teaching Rebecca to speak Gala, employing a linguistic game in which he asks her 'to start a sentence, a narrative, and if she didn't know the right word for what she wanted to say, to substitute another' (p. 249). The results, often ridiculous ('I passed a little house covered with . . . porridge') also yield surprising truths. In the story which Rebecca makes up as she goes along, Bray coaches her through the various kinship terms of Gala. Significantly, in Gala, there is no word for 'home'. Children use 'parents' house', husbands 'the house of my wife'. Rebecca's language lesson therefore also instructs her in African familial structures: 'Yesterday I stayed at the house of my cousin, tomorrow I am going to my (mother's brother) uncle, the day after that I am going to my brother-in-law's' (p. 250). Rehearsing her lesson, Rebecca responds to Bray's flirtatious 'Will you come back to your friend?' (Bray) with the one remaining term: 'Then I will go to the house of my husband'. Since Rebecca has concealed the news of Gordon's impending arrival, the game produces 'something unsaid', breaking a preceding silence. First and foremost the scene indicates the extent to which a new language, a new cultural context, gives the story of Bray and Rebecca its direction and changes its course. In the story necessity (knowing the right word) directs the course of narrative events, as a new language reveals an elided truth. In personal terms, Bray and Rebecca are much exercised by the question of whether they will remain together, return to their spouses' homes or move on, in the migratory relay from one home to another of whites in Africa. In cultural terms, the Gala narrative articulates the various possibilities, and provides the reader with an analogy to the method of Gordimer's novel. Just as Bray committed himself to Shinza on instinctive grounds, so Rebecca finds the right word through an evolving narrative. The episode indicates that Bray and Rebecca are *in* events, participants in an African story rather than selecting out events as anecdotes to be formalized on their own cultural terms.

The political lesson is reinforced on Bray's subsequent visit to Shinza, who now communicates in his own idiom: 'Shinza could move among examples, anecdotes and private thoughts without bothering about sequence, because the links were there, in Bray's mind as in his own' (p. 255). As Shinza forces Bray to rehearse the likely future course of political events, nodding at each point as if 'hearing a lesson by rote', Bray is transformed from mentor to pupil. Just as his persistence forced from Rebecca an avoided fact, so with Shinza, it is drawn out of him that Shinza will use violence to gain his ends, a fact which Bray would much prefer to remain as 'something unsaid'. The evolution of sexual and political plots therefore coincides in the discovery, through an African and non-sequential idiom, of realities wilfully obscured by Bray.

In its denouément the novel enacts the precariousness of any resolution whether in political or personal terms, emphasizing the unstable status of history, ego, and identity. In the confusion of the Gala riots, sparked off by the strikers' anger at 'the failure of authority to protect them' (p. 436) the ironies of

Bray's transitional position are fully revealed. For Bray, 'the habit of authority was instinctive' (p. 437), and he mobilizes with Aleke to disperse the mob. Older linguistic habits also take over. When violence erupts he hears himself bellowing orders, his voice, 'brutally commanding, hard and ringing, a voice dredged up from his racial past, disowning him in the name of sea-captains and slavers between whose legs his genes had been hatched' (p. 444). Yet the suggestion that Bray reverts to paternalism is also undercut. Amidst the 'orgiastic excitement' of the riot Bray seizes a broken bottleneck from a rioter, concealing it in his trousers where it slices deep into his groin. The reassertion of male authority is therefore accompanied by a quasi-emasculation, as Bray is resexualized, desexualized, fighting at Aleke's side, yet hailed by the mob as Shinza's man. Bray's lack of anxiety over the groin injury suggests a self-confidence which transcends merely phallic identity. Indeed after the riot his sexual desire for Rebecca remains in abeyance, in an uncompleted sexual act.

Departing from Gala Bray also leaves behind him 'the patriarchal fig' (p. 456), an age-old tree which has survived many attempts to hack it down, a host to 'teeming parasites whose purpose of existence was to eat it out from within'. Though fertile, the tree is 'at once gigantic and stunted, in senile fecundity endlessly putting out useless fruit on stumps and in crotches' (p. 458). Imagistically the tree suggests both the African country itself, formerly supporting white parasites, now equally threatened by neo-colonialism from within, and, in broader terms, both the durability and the futility of endlessly re-engendered patriarchal structures. Distanced now from senile patriarchy, Bray reflects that 'only for trees is it enough simply to endure; not for human beings' (p. 459). The nature of his death is thus deeply ironic. Halted by a roadblock, a huge tree, Bray is attacked by a mass of smaller men, and finds himself in the ensuing struggle 'desperately hampered by the size and strength of his body' (p. 469). 'Felled' (p. 469) he rises once by brute strength, only to be hacked down again. Though he tries to speak Gala, the words escape him, and he dies with the thought 'I've been interrupted, then —'. In his death both language and the body fail him, each insufficient to counteract the attackers' misreading of him as a white colonialist symbol.

In contrast Rebecca identifies Bray's strength in Reichian terms: 'You don't separate sex and love' (p. 464). For Rebecca, however, Bray's death foregrounds the problematics of any rearrangement of sexual intimacy. She is left squarely confronting her instinctual self. Her reaction to the murder is couched in physical terms: animal howls, followed by a 'physical inkling' (p. 475) of thirst, which she satisfies only to weep at the realization that 'she had begun to live on' (p. 475). At the close of the novel, sexually engorged by regret for the love-making she chose to forgo in Gala, she remains caught in the grip of frightening desire: 'She felt afraid of herself. . . . It would come back, commonplace desire' (p. 500).

Where Rebecca's story is to be continued Bray's is finished and exhibited, summed up in conservative reaction as that of 'a martyr to savages' (p. 503), and as a representative example in a journal devoted to 'The Decline of Liberalism'. Mweta re-edits Bray's papers into the Bray Report, co-opting his ideas to serve expedient ends. Yet though Bray is appropriated, written off in western rhetoric and subsumed to neo-colonialist political norms, the picture remains incomplete. The inadequacy of each version of his story is forcefully revealed in the resistance of his last message, the cryptic paper bearing the codeword, to Rebecca's interpretive attempts. Gazing at its foreign words, Rebecca hunts for a conclusion, a message. Was it merely an aide-memoire? Or destined for her on their separation? Or, 'cracking the code further' (p. 498) a sign that they would remain together? As any phenomenon, Bray's death may be 'read' and classed as a statement, but in the foregrounding of the final mystery of his intentions and achievement Gordimer avoids translating the African experience into conventional literary or political terms. His final words remain unsaid, 'interrupted', his last message unreadable to its recipient.

In an interview, disclaiming an overriding political purpose to her writing in favour of its private and psychological quality, Gordimer commented that: 'Like any other writer my allegiance is to what Proust called "that book of unknown signs within me no one could help me read by any rule".' She concluded that: 'Africa needs an articulated consciousness other than that of newspaper headlines and political speeches.'[23] The point serves as both a fitting conclusion to *A Guest of Honour* and as an apt transition to its successor, *The Conservationist*, which develops Gordimer's awareness of the relation between linguistic and political realities.

3

REALISM DECONSTRUCTED

In contrast to the language of newspaper headlines and political speeches, *The Conservationist* offers the reader another form of articulated consciousness, simultaneously addressing the problems of South African politics and of mimetic realism as a literary mode, by registering the impact of colonialism in terms of language. The point has special importance in the South African context. To write in South Africa is to use only one of many languages, each of them inextricably bound to a class, caste, or race. Language itself is therefore a political statement, a claim to a cultural territory. It follows therefore that the novel throws into sharp relief the intrinsic connections between the conventional representations of realism and the imposition of colonial structures on the land of Africa. If we accept that there is nothing 'real' about realism, that realism is a linguistic creation, a code which fosters an easy, unthinking acceptance of its signs as 'natural', we accept that language may operate on the side of the colonizer. Gordimer's implosion of realism may therefore be read as a first step towards political decolonization. *The Conservationist* therefore renders an internal reality progressively divorced from the reality outside it, the reality of political and ontological consensus. Gordimer employs two principal strategies here: the use of Zulu myth to create a subtext which obliterates the text of the public culture, and the translation of the colonial desire for land into another language, that of sexuality.

Although the foreground of the novel is occupied by Mehring's story, the irruption into the text of excerpts from Henry Callaway's *The Religious System of the Amazulu*[24] introduces another language, that of Zulu culture. The quotations are the organizing points for a subtext which slowly comes into the foreground. The story appears to be that of Mehring, and of the white in South Africa, but reveals itself as that of the blacks. Each quotation introduces or reinforces an event in the novel, surreptitiously at first, later more explicitly.[25] The quotations begin with prayers for corn (p. 35) and for children and the continuation of life (p. 55), to be expected in what is the fourth or fifth year of drought. A further series of quotations (pp. 77, 87, 107) is taken from a dream by one of Callaway's informants,[26] in which he dreams he is awoken and ordered to go down to the river with his brother, there to grapple with a spirit ancestor. This precedes the episode in the novel in which Solomon is awakened in the night, by mysterious figures, supposedly at the behest of his brother, and attacked. Later quotations introduce the image of the 'Amatongo', the ancestors who are beneath the earth (pp. 155, 183)(linked to the dead man buried in the third pasture), the question of material possession of Africa (p. 201), and the bringing of rain and floods by a rainmaker (p. 217) which precedes torrential rain and floods in modern South Africa. The final quotation widens the historical perspective to suggest the enduring occupation of the land by the blacks (p. 233). The effect of these quotations is to suggest that there is a buried logic of fictional events, which may be expressed in the rhetoric of myth.

From the black point of view the main events in the compound in the year during which the action takes place are: the drought, the discovery of the body in the pasture, the attack on Solomon, the fire, the spirit-possession of Phineas's wife, with its attendant feast and dance, the flood, and finally the reburial of the dead man, as the cycle of the seasons completes itself.

This subtext, buried like the black man, rises to the surface of the novel and repossesses it, obliterating the 'paper' possession of Mehring and his story. The dead man is discovered in a reed bed. His body 'isn't actually on the earth at all, but held slightly above it on a nest of reeds it has flattened. . . . The only injury he shows is a long red scratch, obviously made by a sharp broken reed' (p. 14). The situation refers explicitly to a myth of origins. In *The Religious System of the Amazulu* Callaway points out that the cult of ancestors is connected with a bed of reeds. A father is the 'uthlanga' or ancestor of his children; from him they broke off. 'Uthlanga' is a reed, one which is capable of throwing out offsets and is therefore metaphorically a source of being. One of Callaway's informants, who took 'uthlanga' literally, stated that man came from a bed of reeds.[27] The nest of reeds also suggests the guinea fowl, which Mehring is trying to conserve; the novel opens with the image of guinea fowl eggs, offered by children who have made a nest for themselves in the grass. From the outset, therefore, the fundamental questions of the novel – Who shall inherit Africa? How shall it be conserved? – are set out in terms of Zulu myth.

The cursory burial of the dead black conditions later events. The first of these is the attack on Solomon, who is discovered unconscious on the veld. As accounts of the attack become ritualized, the legend grows 'that he was attacked in the night by a spirit: there was something down there at the third pasture' (p. 85). In realistic terms, Solomon has been beaten up for non-payment of debts. Symbolically he has failed to pay a debt to his culture.

The fire which follows centres upon the third pasture, but also appears to have gone through the compound, though Mehring dismisses the blackened earth as merely the ash from braziers. In Zulu practice, however, rainmakers burn the earth around their homes in the belief that the god, seeing the black area, knows that the rainmaker is seeking rain. In Zulu myth it is the lightning bird which brings rain, touching the grass with fire. Rainmakers therefore sacrifice colourful birds in the belief that, as drought takes colour from the land, the killing of colour (e.g. the rainbow-feathered hornbill) will cause the sky to weep.[28] In the novel, when rain does come, it is described as a bird: 'taking off again with a sweep that shed, monstrous cosmic peacock, gross paillettes of hail, a dross of battering rain' (p. 218). Drought, the dead black, fire and the images of the rainbird are carefully organized into a coherent pattern of Zulu belief.

The fire is followed by the account of the feast celebrating the initiation of Phineas's wife as a spirit medium. The account of her possession follows the pattern of Zulu possession, as documented by Callaway. The underlying idea is that ancestors are tormenting the subject, complaining that he or she is no longer true to their culture. Interestingly, spirit possession is more common among Zulu women than men. S. G. Lee's sociological study stresses this point: 'To become diviners is for pagan Zulu women the only socially recognized way of escape from an impossible situation in family life; it is also the only way an outstanding woman can win general social prestige.'[29] Social power is gained by the possessed person who is given presents and feasts, ostensibly for the spirits. It is associated with sexual and family conflicts (lack of children, an engagement to marry which is resisted, confusion of goals at the menopause). Phineas's wife 'had no living children', is 'somewhere around the end of the childbearing age' (p. 156) and no longer sleeps with her husband. By becoming a diviner, therefore, the woman escapes from the pressures of her culture and her sex. In her ravings Phineas's wife conjures up visions of flood and her initiation precedes the actual flood which is seen as a female revenge:'The weather came from the Moçambique Channel. Space is conceived of as trackless but there are beats about the world frequented by cyclones given female names' (p. 218). One of these hits South Africa, washing the ground clean of the fire ashes, unearthing the dead man, and regenerating the burnt area.

In the final scene of the novel the conflicts appear to be resolved. 'Phineas's wife was at peace, there was no burden of spirits on her shoulders' (p. 252). In the background to the unnamed black's funeral stand the female members of the sect of Zion, a breakaway from orthodox Christianity, in which Christian tenets have been adapted to indigenous patterns of thought. The close of the novel therefore offers a quasi-resolution of white and indigenous cultures. The unconscious life of the woman shapes formally her actions in society. Through Zulu myth Gordimer gives formal shape to the novel, articulating a very different consciousness from that of the public rhetoric of South Africa. In the language of Zulu culture, possession is non-material, passive, a means of resolving social and sexual conflicts.[30] The divination cult offers a therapy for social deprivation, a catharsis for the Zulu woman in a subservient role. One meaning of the title has thus been indicated: the blacks conserve their beliefs, and their beliefs conserve and regenerate the land and its people.

It is significant that it is a woman who comes to express Zulu culture and to resolve its problems. The conjunction of woman and land is repeated in the events of the foreground. Phineas's wife may have achieved some independent status in her society, but the other women are visibly getting the worst of it. Dawood's Indian wife longs for Durban, Mehring's mistress is forced to flee, the Portuguese immigrant girl is molested, even the Afrikaner daughter-in-law and grand-daughters of old De Beer are thoroughly cowed. The point being made here is not merely a feminist one. Female exploitation and exploitation of the land are linked; sexual guilt functions as a surrogate for colonial guilts.

The fantasy-ideal form of Mehring's relationship to woman and land occurs in an incident on board a plane. Returning from a business trip, Mehring is forced to travel tourist class, and during the night engages in sexual play with his neighbour, a young Portuguese immigrant girl. The scene may be read as an example of Mehring's sexual colonialism; no woman is safe from his hand or eye. Mehring's mind moves into the event through his perceptions of the land below him, which he sees as 'soft lap after lap' of sand and desert. The opening phrase 'Golden reclining nudes of the desert' (p. 120) refers as much to the dunes as to any sunning tourist. The body of the girl becomes the land, as Mehring locates it, explores, explicitly compares its flesh to water in the desert, experiences the 'grain' of the skin, and moves over the terrain, exploring the ridges of her anatomy. The plane, an enclosed world outside time and place, veiled in sandstorms, allows Mehring to ignore social, sexual, and class taboos. The events are 'happening nowhere' (p. 123). Moreover, Mehring's colonialism extends to the whole of reality. The closed world of the plane communicates an impression of consciousness operating in a void, dissociated in its private world from the world beneath, annihilating reality. Beneath him the desert sand becomes 'an infinite progression of petrified sound waves' (p. 125), which he watches while caressing the girl, equally soundless, echoing back to him his own activity. Sexual activity is described here as linguistic, as a monologue, delicate phrasing, delicate questioning, and finally entry into the 'soundless O of the little mouth' (p. 124). The relationship goes on and on in an endless night of solipsistic communication which does not advance, merely making Mehring hyper-aware of 'the bounds of himself'. The entire scene is rather like a negative image of Bray's relationship with Rebecca. Where Bray and Rebecca moved towards an African reality, linguistic and political, Mehring remains confined within his own vision of reality. The erotic quality of the experience is fundamentally auto-erotic, the girl utterly passive. In the method of narration, infinitely oblique, the question, 'Who spoke first? Was it at all sure that it was he?' (p. 121) goes unanswered, even unasked. The girl's body 'takes up the narrative', Mehring's hand 'took up the thread of communication' (p. 122) but there is no actual utterance. The two collaborate in a surreptitious relationship, never fully articulated, relying upon the convention that they are utterly separate beneath their airline rugs, while in fact enjoying a close intimacy. Their relationship is 'Not without tenderness, but who is ever to know that is part of the scandal' (p. 125), just as Mehring's relation to his land and his 'boys' is not without tenderness but none the less a scandal. Sexual fantasy as a surrogate for colonial lusts is extended in ontological terms here. As a white South African male, Mehring's relationship to women can only be a form of slumming, even without crossing the race or class lines. As such, his activity can give him back only his own image. The sterile desert beneath confirms this reading of the scene, 'echoing itself since there was no organic renewal by which life could be measured' (p. 125). White solipsism prevents change and renewal of the external world. Another culture, beyond Mehring's, carries the burden of renewal and rebirth.

Mehring's activities on the plane are presented as a flashback, framed by two images of fathers and sons, the Indians whose shop is near the farm, and the visit of Mehring's own son, Terry. The first episode takes place in an enclosed space, a circumscribed world, akin to Mehring's plane. The Indians' shop is surrounded by dogs in a ring of savagery, behind a stockade which Bismillah continually repairs, a conservationist of a more defensive kind. The image of a culture deliberately walling itself in, refusing to communicate across the lines drawn by apartheid, even collaborating with it, is also an image of walled-off consciousness. When the stockade doors are opened, for example, the dogs do not escape, 'as if for them, the pattern of closed gates was still barred across their eyes' (p. 119). Mind-forged manacles, psychological constraints, operate even more repressively than external ones. Within the house Dawood and his young bride are seen crammed into one room with her dowry furniture, a further space within a space, a space which Dawood sees as paradise. His father comments: 'The boy will be happy anywhere where he can be touching the first woman he has all to himself. Anywhere. The room is paradise' (p. 112). In the Indians' shop the closed world does not intersect in any meaningful way with the world of the customers. Bismillah, conversing in Gujerati with his father, enjoys total privacy. To the blacks he employs 'the semantics of the trade' (p. 113) saying one thing to mean another, cagily unwilling to say more than the bare minimum. The rhythm of their speech is not unlike the rhythm of

61

Mehring's 'conversation' on the plane: 'Demand. Response. Counterdemand. Statement.' (p. 113). When Dorcas's husband challenges Bismillah, Bismillah deliberately distances him, communicating through another, though Dorcas's husband is perfectly intelligible. The incident demonstrates how each closed culture mimics the one above it, absorbing and passing on the aggression. Bismillah is thinking aloud at this point, imagining Mehring's probable reaction to a business proposition: 'And go to hell, and who you bloody think you are' (p. 116). But the words are voiced, directed at Dorcas's husband. The episode dramatizes the lack of consensus in South Africa, the separate existence of different codes and circumscribed worlds which communicate only crudely, underhandedly, or with violence.

The visit of Terry, Mehring's son, presents Mehring's separate peace in another guise, that of exile. Terry's rucksack, with its peace symbol, looms large in the enclosed space of Mehring's car. The action again centres on problems of sexuality and of communication. Beneath the text of the conversation an ominous silence echoes. Father and son appear to speak different languages: 'Were they referring to the same things when they talked together?' (p. 128). Neither engages with the real subject, Terry's impending military service. The conversation begins beside a sign in three languages, 'NO THOROUGHFARE GEEN TOEGANG AKUNANDLELA LAPHA' (p. 134) and progresses only as far as a dead end in the fields. At one point, Mehring considers Terry's use of the term 'Namibia'. 'Why that and not another invention expressive of a certain attitude towards the place?' (p. 132). Terry favours Namibia as a neutral term, which will not suggest that the land belongs to any of the peoples occupying it. Language attempts to say nothing here, to be neutral, an impossible task. Terry's conversation with his father also remains a neutral surface. The rhythm of the passage is a continued attempt and failure to guess the unspoken thoughts of the other, and to trap him into revelation. Mehring seizes upon Terry's book, published by the Campaign For Homosexual Equality, as a possible answer, a reality beneath their speech: 'Is this the subject?' (p. 145). Whether Terry is, or is not, homosexual remains uncertain, though in Mehring's terms he might as well be. Attraction to Africa and to woman are so identified that rejection of the one implies rejection of the other.

A further irony is present. The book is 'hidden away like the goat' (p. 145) whose bones are used in Zulu divining. This method of divination is question-and-answer, slight nuances of emphasis in the answerer's replies finally yielding the 'correct' response. Terry and his father lack even this subtlety. The book when found is just another inscrutable surface, a mish-mash of legalese jargon and 'text-book mumbo-jumbo'. Mehring penetrates beneath neutral surface conversation only to find an even more 'public', social rhetoric. Terry's withdrawal from the enclosed 'private' world of South Africa makes him a creature of a neutralized empty world, the desert of Namibia rather than the paradise of Dawood's room or Mehring's plane. No medium connects subjective paradise and objective desert. White Africa is caught in a double-bind: between Mehring, the conservationist who conserves only the mapped out landscape of his own mind, and Terry the objective, socially-conscious inhabitant of a neutral desert.

In *The Conservationist*, however, the natural landscape is as resistant to realism as to rhetoric. As a result of the fire, which leaves particles of smoke in the air, it is blurred and softened. Drought has a similar effect. 'Dust has the effect on his distant hills of a pencil sketch gone over with a soft rubber' (p. 101). The cyclone, in particular, dissolves the normal landscape, and this is associated with a social change. When the road is washed away, Mehring is separated from the farm and the Africans have to cope without him. It is as though he were dead. Jacobus opens cupboards, 'as possessions must be sorted after a death, putting objects aside like words in a code or symbols of a life that will never be understood coherently, never explained now' (p. 224). Gordimer offers here a vision of Africa without the white man – and at the same time she offers a different form of vision. Rain dissolves the normal paths and ways of society, washing out both social domination and a way of seeing. In the rain, 'The sense of perspective was changed' (p. 219). Car tyres behave as if greased 'engaging with a tangible surface only on intermittent revolutions' (p. 219). Within the cars children shriek with joy and fear 'at the lack of sensation – the impression of being carried along without any kind of familiar motion'. Gordimer's language conveys the same excitement, engaging with a tangible surface only intermittently, carrying the reader along in a motion which operates beneath the level of consciousness, leaving realism and a familiar social consensus behind. At those points where the rhetoric of Zulu culture intersects with that of the 'foreground' action the perspective of the text is changed, dissolves. The reader is uncertain which action is primary, which 'background'. When a car is washed away in the flood, Gordimer's own account – 'It was seen to float a moment and then engage with some solid surface again – just as it was about to gain the rise, something burst out there' (p. 220) – is contrasted with the public rhetoric of the newspapers, with their nine-year-old photographs of Mr and Mrs Loftus Coetzee, vanished 'without a trace before the horrified eyes of astonished witnesses' (p. 221). White rhetoric is washed away now, matter flows and language changes, and all the reader's normal certainties collapse.

Nowhere is reality more in question than in the final pages of the novel. The reader grasps for a tangible surface in the events occurring between Mehring and the anonymous woman, his 'death' which is not a death, and the mysterious figure in the background of the picnic place. Mehring's mind appears to have lost its grip on reality shortly before. After having coffee with a friend's daughter, a girl he lusts after, news reaches him that her father has gassed himself, as the result of a financial scandal. Mehring's reaction is obsessively guilty: 'It's me. Drawn up, he has been seized, he is going to be confronted, at last' (p. 184). The words 'It's me' are the daughter's unspoken greeting (p. 179), the words of his arrested mistress on the telephone, and the horrid spectre of the Portuguese girl, challenging him. The train of associations leads Mehring to confront the colonial guilt beneath the sexual, as the coffee he's just drunk turns to poison: 'Some of them take poison. A dose of cyanide, it's quicker' (p. 185). The phrase 'It's me' refers also to Mehring, equally implicated in the financial scandal of South Africa, equally guilty. Cyanide, he recalls, is 'the stuff that is used in the most effective and cheapest process for extracting gold from the auriferous reef. . . . It is what makes yellow the waste that is piled up . . . where the road first leaves the city' (p. 185).

The dénouement of the novel situates Mehring in the same symbolic landscape, an overgrown rubbish dump between mounds of cyanide waste. The scene reiterates and unites the themes of the novel. The car journey takes Mehring through a landscape which functions as a mental topography. Mehring is no longer responding to normal signs. He has 'an awful moment of looking at a green light and not knowing what it means. Jeers of horns are prodding at him. Blank' (p. 237). He clings to familiar landmarks in an attempt to hang on to his vision of reality, picking out bus stops: 'ticking off a familiar progression of objects can be used to restore concentration' (p. 238). Although the woman hitchhiker is once again a representative of the land she is not a paradise conserved, but an ecological disaster. Her face is like a cyanide dump. 'The grain of the skin is gigantic, muddy and coarse. A moon surface. Grey-brown with layers of muck that don't cover the blemishes' (p. 246). In her person she sums up all the women of the book. She babbles like a schoolgirl, reminds Mehring of his mistress, has an accent which suggests she could be Afrikaans-speaking or Portuguese. She may even be black: 'That hair's been straightened and that sallowness isn't sunburn' (p. 247). Mehring's abandonment of her prefigures abandonment of Africa.

> He's going to leave her to them . . . he's going to make a dash for it, a leap, sell the place to the first offer. . . . He's going to run, run and leave them to rape her and rob her. She'll be all right. They survive everything. Coloured or poor-white,

whichever she is, their brothers or fathers take their virginity good and early. They can have it, the whole four hundred acres. (p. 250)

As Mehring is about to possess the woman he becomes aware of a pair of male legs in the background. Two possibilities are entertained here: the man is a thug in conspiracy with the girl to rob him, or he is a policeman enforcing the laws against interracial sex. On the level of Mehring's subconscious he is the Freudian censor, interrupting his sexual activities. On the political level he recalls the police at the start of the novel, who bury the murdered black 'as you might fling a handful of earth on the corpse of a rat' (p. 248). 'Dispose of the body and so you dump your rubbish on somebody's private property' (p. 249). The black man, the body, the body of woman, and the rubbish dumps form one massive image of colonial guilt. Mehring is in the reverse position to Phineas's wife. Her unconscious life shapes her society. His unconscious life is formally shaped and repressed by his society. The final words of the chapter are those of other people inside Mehring's head: 'Come and look, they're all saying. What is it? Who is it? It's Mehring. It's Mehring down there' (p. 250).

The problems the passage poses for the reader hinge upon the question: What is real? Which is the accepted version of events? Has a well-meaning white been murdered by black thugs? Or, has he been arrested by a repressive regime? Has he, as an industrialist, been developing a country? Or is he guilty of abandoning it to industrial rape and despoilment? These fictional problems are precisely the problems posed by South Africa – a lack of normality, shared language or vision. To be true to a political situation Gordimer has to avoid translating events into the realism of a materialist society. Mehring, at the end of the novel, seizes upon the detail of the mysterious man's comb in his sock.

If it were not for the comb – so undeniably the sort of detail that no unnerved imagination could supply – there could not possibly be anyone there. There cannot be anyone there. But there is. Someone has been there all the time. (p. 246)

66

Even realistic detail functions within the nightmare, confirming its horror, rather than mapping out a safe certainty. The novel ends with the re-interment of the dead black, the 'someone' who has been there all the time and now takes final possession.

In *The Conservationist* Gordimer explores an individual white consciousness without giving that consciousness final narrative and political authority. Although woman and black man function as symbols in the white subconscious, onto whom the conflicts of the white psyche are projected, such fantasy projection is critically examined and set in a different perspective by the foregrounding of the black consciousness, rising from its buried position to the surface of the text. Under her ironic title, Gordimer argues that to conserve the land, to maintain it as neither the hothouse of fantasy, nor the desert of neutral tones, the first task is to regenerate its language. A new rhetoric expresses rather than represses the individual, and the land possesses as much as it is possessed.

4

PROSPERO'S COMPLEX

Gordimer followed *The Conservationist* with *Burger's Daughter*, a more overtly political novel. Gordimer has remarked that all South African novels, whatever their political intentions, involve the problem of racism: 'There is no country in the Western world where the creative imagination, whatever it seizes upon, finds the focus of even the most private event set in the social determination of racial laws.'[31] There are, however, those who have argued that the white South African novelist is automatically corrupted by a privileged position, that Gordimer's audience can only be other privileged whites, and that the products of her imagination are therefore intrinsically a part of a racist society.[32] That society none the less saw itself very clearly as the target of *Burger's Daughter*, as the banning of the novel, the reaction of the South African censors, and the ensuing international furore, bore witness.[33] Gordimer is well aware of the charges against the white novelist in South Africa, and designs her novel as an examination of the accusation that her art is solipsistic, that the white can produce only an art which articulates the dominating force of the white imagination.

Rosa Burger begins her tale with the frank recognition that 'One is never talking to oneself, always one is addressed to someone . . . even dreams are performed before an audience' (p. 16). In *Burger's Daughter* Gordimer focuses upon the fantasies of the white subconscious, in order to undermine their power. Once again a body lies below the level of consciousness, here the body of a white woman. In the opening scene of the novel Rosa is presented as she appears to other observers, as seen by casual passers-by, as reported on by her headmistress, and as transformed by the rhetoric of the Left, which converts her into 'Little Rosa Burger', 'an example to us all' (p. 12). The later Rosa reflects upon her invisibility as a person: 'When they saw me outside the prison what did they see? I shall never know. . . . I saw – see that profile in a hand-held mirror directed towards another mirror' (pp. 13–14). As the daughter of a Communist hero, it is assumed by others that Rosa's views reflect her father's. Rosa is thus trapped in a hall of mirrors, an object in the eyes of others, her internal reality unknown. A figure in an ideological landscape, she is placed by observers only in relation to their own political position: an image of the struggle in the 'bland heroics of badly written memoirs by the faithful' (p. 14), a suspicious object to state surveillance. This public rhetoric of South Africa contrasts, in the opening scene, with a bleeding body, invisible to all shades of South African opinion. For Rosa these external views are eclipsed by the pains of puberty: 'real awareness is all focussed in the lower part of my pelvis . . . outside the prison the internal landscape of my mysterious body turns me inside out' (p. 15). In the novel Rosa's sexuality is the basis of an exploration of the racist psyche. The disjunction between external and internal realities is rendered in the form of the novel, in the alternation of first- and third-person narratives, which interact in order to explore the roots of racism.

Burger's Daughter poses the question of racism as primary or secondary phenomenon. Is racism the product of a political system (capitalism) as Lionel Burger would argue? Or is racism a screen for more primary sexual insecurities? The central images of the novel are drawn from an informed awareness of the principal arguments involved here. Racism has been generally understood by various commentators as a product of sexual repression. In his early, classic study Gordon Allport[34] notes that to the white the Negro appears dark, mysterious, and distant, yet at the same time warm, human, and potentially accessible. These elements of mystery and forbiddenness are present in sex appeal in a Puritanical society. Sex is forbidden, blacks are forbidden; the ideas begin to fuse. White racism expresses itself in response to ambivalence towards the body, conceived of as both attractive and repugnant. Joel Kovel[35] developed the argument, describing aversive racism as the product of anal repressions. In his view the Negro is not the actual basis of racism but a surrogate or substitute. In white culture bodily products are seen as dirt. The white therefore splits the universe into good (clean, white, spiritual) and bad (dirty, black, material). Things associated with the sensual body are dirty; those things which may be seen as non-sensuous are clean. Racism therefore depends upon the displacement of 'dirty' activities onto an alter ego. Fantasies of dirt underlie racism, which is a product of sexual repressions.

Octave Mannoni's analysis,[36] in *Prospero and Caliban*, places greater emphasis on sexual fantasy, arguing that colonial racism simply brings to the surface traits buried in the European psyche, repressed in Europe but manifest in the colonial experience. Colonial countries are the nearest approach possible to the archetype of the desert island. Colonial life is a substitute life available to those who are obscurely drawn to a world of fantasy projection, a childish world without real people. For Mannoni, European man is always in inner conflict between the need for attachments which offer emotional security, and the need for complete individualization. Revolt against parents is an important factor here. When a child suffers because he feels that the ties between him and his parents are threatened, the child also feels guilt, because he would also like to break those ties. He therefore dreams of a world without bonds, into which he can project the untrammelled images of his unconscious. This desire to break every attachment is impossible in fact. But it is realized by the colonial when he goes into a 'primitive' society, a society which seems less 'real' than his own. The more remote people are, the easier they appear to attract our projections. Prospero's relation with Caliban and Ariel, Crusoe's with Friday, are cases in point. In *July's People* a similar relationship obtains between white woman and black servant. In the literature of colonialism, the native woman is more commonly a focus for this type of projection. For the white colonial her personality is so little externalized that it acts as a mirror to his projections. He may then live happily amidst them, without granting that the Other has autonomous existence: 'It is himself a man is looking for when he goes far away; near at hand he is liable to come up against others. Far-away princesses are psychologically important in this respect' (Mannoni, p. 111). As will become evident, Rosa Burger almost becomes identified with the image of the far-away princess, though in her case, Europe becomes the magic island, and her guilty revolt against her father is only temporary.

In this connection Mannoni's analysis of the roots of racism in a patriarchal system is particularly important. For Mannoni the opposition between Caliban and Prospero in *The Tempest* hinges upon Miranda's presence as the only woman on the island. Having first treated the black (Caliban) as his son, Prospero later accuses him of attempting to rape Miranda, and subsequently enslaves him. In short, Prospero justifies his hatred of Caliban on grounds of sexual guilt. Analysing the 'Prospero complex' Mannoni draws a picture of the paternalist colonial whose racism is a way of rationalizing guilty incestuous feelings. In his view the sexual basis of racism is revealed in the old cliché of the racist: But would you let your daughter marry one? Uneasy incestuous feelings in the father are disturbed by this argument. For Mannoni it is easy to see why it is always a daughter, sister, or neighbour's wife, never his own, whom a man imagines in this situation. When a white man imagines a white woman as violated by a black man he is seeking to rid himself of guilt by projecting his thoughts onto another (Caliban), putting the blame for his 'dirty' sexuality onto somebody else. In *The Tempest* Prospero's departure

71

from the colonial island is accompanied by his renunciation of his art, in this case magical arts which enable him to dominate a world created in his own image. There are clearly interesting connections here with the character of Baasie (adopted as a son by Lionel Burger but later abandoned), with Rosa's relationship with her father, and with the nature of Gordimer's art.

Mannoni's is, of course, a highly ambivalent analysis of the colonial enterprise. Socialists, in particular, have denounced the search for psychological solutions as merely providing an alibi for those who refuse to confront political problems. Frantz Fanon contested Mannoni in detail. While allowing that the 'civilized' white may retain an irrational longing for areas of repressed sexuality which he then projects onto the Negro, he argues that this image of the sexual-sensual-genital black can be corrected: 'The eye is not merely a mirror, but a correcting mirror. The eye should make it possible for us to correct cultural errors.'[37] For Fanon sexuality need not remain at the level of frustration, inauthenticity or projection. True authentic love is 'wishing for others what one postulates for oneself' (Fanon, p. 41). Confrontation of one's psychic drives is only a necessary part of a process of cultural evolution:

The tragedy of the man is that he was once a child. It is through the effort to recapture the self and to scrutinize the self, it is through the lasting tension of their freedom that man will be able to create the ideal conditions for a human world. . . . Was my freedom not given to me in order to build the world of the *You*? (Fanon, pp. 231–2)

Burger's Daughter charts just such a process of self-scrutiny. Rosa remembers and observes her past self in an extensive attempt to recapture and reconstitute it, and to engage with the world of the 'You'. Rosa's first-person narrative is directed to three people, each addressed as 'You': Conrad, a surrogate brother with whom she enjoys childish erotic freedom, Katya, a sexually permissive replacement mother, and finally Lionel

Burger, the father to whom she eventually returns. 'You' is obviously also the reader who is initiated into these three identities. The reader participates in the fantasy while also measuring the difference between these surrogate people and himself. At key points Gordimer adopts Fanon's terminology. For Conrad, the significant dynamic is 'the tension between creation and destruction in yourself' (p. 47). Rosa describes Lionel antithetically: 'the tension that makes it possible to live lay, for him, between self and others' (p. 86). In the novel Gordimer's narrative technique draws the reader into a tension of freedom, progressing from Conrad's inner psychological existence to a fresh orientation towards the world of the autonomous other. The alternation between first- and third-person narrative creates a tension between external image and internal voice, between 'she' and 'I'. As 'You' the reader continually mediates the two, correcting the errors of the eye, emerging from the spell of the internal voice. The reader is therefore offered a choice: to place the voice addressing him as initiating him into a secret intimacy, or to refuse to identify with a surrogate 'You' and thus register the possibility of a world in which communication is not limited to depersonalized stereotypes.

In the first movement of the novel Rosa Burger disowns her original attachments in order to enter a world in which surrogate mothers and brothers replace them in a fantasy landscape. She does so largely as a result of ambivalence towards the body as one example will indicate. When Rosa meets Marisa Kgosana in a shop, their embrace is described as a step through the looking glass:

> To enter for a moment the invisible magnetic field of the body of a beautiful creature and receive on oneself its imprint – breath misting and quickly fading on a glass pane – this was to immerse in another mode of perception. (p. 134)

To the salesgirl Marisa appears in the image of the sensuous black woman, distant and unreal. She asks, 'Where's she from? One of those French islands?' (p. 139). Marisa, however, has returned, not from the exotic Seychelles or Mauritius, but from Robben Island, the prison to which white racist attitudes have banished her husband. From Marisa Rosa's mind moves at once to Baasie, remembered quite differently as a creature of darkness and dirt. Rosa remembers Baasie wetting the bed which they shared as children: 'In the morning the sheets were cold and smelly. I told tales to my mother – Look what Baasie's done in his bed! – but in the night I didn't know whether this warmth ... came from him or me' (pp. 138–40). Quite obviously the two images suggest the twin racist strategies delineated by Kovel and Mannoni – the attempt to use blackness as a way to sensual liberation (Marisa), the attempt to blame 'dirty' actions on the black (Baasie). Rosa exists in tension between these two forms of racism, but it is a tension transformed by Gordimer's art into a political challenge. Key terms and images – island paradise, incestuous desires, projection onto mirrors, far-away princesses – recur, as do images of dirt, guilt, bodily products, and repugnance. The language of racism is exploited, however, in order to confront the reader with a series of questions. Which version of Rosa do we accept? That of a white woman who is part of a racist society and who can address a 'You' who exists only in her own projections? Or that of a woman confronting and correcting a stereotyped image and painfully learning to address herself to a world of other autonomous beings? Arguably, the narrative art of *Burger's Daughter* refuses to maintain the text at the level of private fantasy or dream, and also avoids the danger of the depersonalized image. Gordimer employs the terms of the white racist subconscious in an attempt to free her art from Prospero's complex, and to direct it towards a world where 'You' is not a fantasy projection but real.

Gordimer's daring strategy, here, is to select as the focus of the novel a white woman attempting to achieve autonomy by emerging from her father's dominance. As the daughter of a white Afrikaner Communist, Rosa is an extremely complex figure. She may be defined in terms of sex, race, and position in the class struggle, and thus encapsulates the warring explana-

74

tions of South African racism. In order to assert her autonomy Rosa can rebel only against another rebel. Her father is fighting political repression so to fight his psychological influence is to join with the forces of political repression. This paradoxical situation, a variant on the concern with authoritarian fathers in *A Guest of Honour*, is made evident from the beginning. In the eyes of the faithful, Rosa is desexualized and infantilized, maintained in the image of the faithful daughter. In the opening scene Rosa is described as having already 'taken on her mother's role in the household' (p. 12), 'giving loving support' (p. 12) to her father. In the Burger household the children have few exclusive rights with their parents for whom intimate personal relationships are subordinate to the struggle. As a young woman Rosa gains her parents' approval by posing as the fiancée of Noel de Witt, a device to enable him to receive visits in prison. Decked out, scented, 'a flower standing for what lies in her lap' (p. 68) Rosa presents herself as a sexual object in prison, conveying a political subtext beneath innocuous lovey-dovey phrases. Rosa's parents are blind to the fact that she *is* actually in love with Noel. They are happy to cast her in a surrogate sexual role, which denies the reality of her emotions and confines her sexuality within prison walls. In the overall action of the novel Rosa moves from prison to prison. Infantilized as 'Little Rosa Burger' at the start, she becomes in the final pages once more a child. Flora describes her at the end: 'She looked like a little girl. . . . About fourteen' (p. 360). In the eyes of the faithful Rosa has not changed at all. She is still her father's daughter, and is living out the historical destiny prepared for her by him. Imagistically the prison is connected to the dichotomy of 'inside' and 'outside' in the novel. The reader, with access to Rosa's internal voice, knows that Rosa defected from her father in a belated revolt against the ideology of the parental generation. Does Rosa return from France to continue the political struggle, making a free choice on the basis of internal understanding? Or has Rosa simply fled from the erotic life of Europe in order to return to a desexualized security, a prison of women where she is once more her father's daughter? Rosa is finally imprisoned on suspicion of abetting the schoolchildren's revolt – a revolt informed by consciousness of black brotherhood and directed against paternalism, whether white or black. Her return follows her encounter with Baasie who denies her 'brotherhood'. In external political terms the white is rejected by blacks and retreats into paternalism. In internal psychological terms, however, the position is more complex.

That Rosa's rejection of her father is connected with sexual assertion is indicated in the scene with Clare Terblanche, daughter of Dick and Ivy who have been as surrogate parents to Rosa. Rosa is tempted by the parental warmth of their welcome and recognizes their attraction: 'In the enveloping acceptance of Ivy's motherly arms – she feels as if I were her own child – there is expectance, even authority. To her warm breast one could come home again and do as you said I would, go to prison' (p. 114). Clare Terblanche lives with her parents and her life is devoted to their cause. As a result she is desexualized. Clare appears at Rosa's door as a shadow which 'had no identity' (p. 118) glimpsed through a glass panel. In Rosa's eyes, Clare is still her childish playmate, sturdy as a teddy-bear, suffering from eczema and knock knees which went uncorrected by parents for whom the body is unimportant. Where Rosa's is a body with 'the assurance of embraces' (p. 121) Clare, faithful to her father's ideals, has 'a body that had no signals' (p. 122). Clare's purpose here is to recruit Rosa as a political intermediary. Rosa refuses on the grounds that she will not conform to her parents' image of her: 'Other people break away. They live completely different lives. Parents and children don't understand each other. . . . Not us. We live as they lived' (p. 127). One event specifically links Clare to the earlier Rosa. When Rosa shows Clare the vacant apartment, Clare discovers a used sanitary towel in a cupboard. As they leave she removes this unmentionable object to the waste-bin 'and buried her burden . . . as if she had successfully disposed of a body' (p. 129). Disposing of a body is, of course, exactly what Clare has done. Supposedly involved with the people's struggle, her background isolates her from the realities of the body. Irony cuts both ways here, however. In the background a radio announcer is 'reciting with the promiscuous intimacy of his medium a list of birthday, anniversary and lover's greetings for military trainees on border duty' (p. 119). Rosa's refusal to help Clare aligns her with this promiscuous intimacy. In South Africa there appears to be no possible mediation between the desexualized image and an erotic intimacy which is the voice of the repressive state.

This erotic intimacy is developed in the person of Brandt Vermeulen. Breaking her attachments to the original family, Rosa sets out to obtain a passport, aligning herself with an alternative family. In order to defect, she makes a series of visits to Afrikaners 'whose history, blood and language made [Lionel] their brother' (p. 173). Of them all, she selects as her ally Brandt Vermeulen, member of the Broederbond, the Afrikaner political 'brotherhood' which runs South Africa from within Parliament. Brandt's house expresses the psychological reality of colonialism. The facade is that of a Boer farmhouse of seventy or eighty years ago. Within, however, all the internal walls have been demolished to create one large space of comfortable intimacy, with glass walls giving access to a secret garden. Behind the facade of historical legitimacy there exists a vast personal space, inhabited by the erotic male. Brandt runs an art publishing house and is about to produce a book of erotic poems and woodcuts. By participating in a racist political system Brandt has found sexual liberation. Rosa's attempt to escape from her father has brought her to a 'brother' whose facade of reverence for the traditions of his fathers conceals a sophistic eroticism. The room is dominated by a sculpture, a perspex torso of a woman's body, set upon a colonial chest. Described as suggesting both the ice of frigidity and the hardness of tumescence the sculpture presents an image of erotic woman as a reified object of display, possessed by the male and existing only in his internal space. It is on this erotic object that Brandt's more 'sophisticated' art depends, as Prospero's art draws upon a complex of sexual motives. In the garden a small black boy plays, amidst chairs spattered with messy bird-droppings, indicating *his* place in Brandt's internal landscape. To escape desexualization by a father, Rosa has entered a landscape organized by a surrogate brother to reflect his own fantasy.

Conrad is another such 'brother'. (The watchman for whom he places bets describes him to Rosa at one point as 'Your brother': p. 149.) Rosa's relation with Conrad is foreshadowed in the visit she pays to the Nels' farm when first separated from her jailed parents. At the farm 'More and more, she based herself in the two rooms marked Strictly Private – Streng Privaat' (p. 55). On the door hangs a wooden clock-face on which visitors mark the time of their call. To Rosa it is 'immediately recognizable to any child as something from childhood's own system of signification. Beyond any talisman is a private world unrelated to and therefore untouched by what is lost or gained' (p. 55). The dummy clock marks the entrance to the timeless world of the child's psyche, a place to which Rosa returns when separated from her parents. The visit to the Nels also marks the disappearance from Rosa's life of Baasie, who then becomes timeless, existing only in her memory. When Rosa is permanently separated from her parents, she sets up house with Conrad in a world also outside time and place. Their cottage, soon to be demolished in favour of a new freeway, is let without official tenure at 'an address that no longer existed' (p. 21). Set in a jungle of palms, the house is 'safe and cosy as a child's playhouse and sexually arousing as a lovers' hideout. It was nowhere' (p. 21). In the dark of their secret cottage, Conrad and Rosa act out their dreams of a private erotic world in which parents are no longer controlling. For Conrad, a man with no political affiliations, only psychological events matter. Sharpeville passes unnoticed, eclipsed by the awareness that his mother has a lover. Freed from his Oedipal conflicts by the awareness that his mother was no longer the sole possession of his father, Conrad became obsessed with her. 'I was mad about her; now I could be, with someone other than my father there already' (p. 44). Rosa

78

admits a kinship with Conrad: 'We had in common such terrible secrets in the tin house: you can fuck your mother and wish your father dead' (p. 63). Conrad's reaction to Lionel's death is 'Now you are free'. Freedom from the father liberates Rosa sexually but is attended by guilt. She wished for this freedom. She obtained it on her father's death. She concludes, 'I know I must have wished him to die' (p. 63). In the psyche there is no distinction between what she has actually done and what she has imagined. This criminality of the imagination is seen as liberating by Conrad, who quotes Jung in his support: 'One day when he was a kid Jung imagined God sitting up in the clouds and shitting on the world below. His father was a pastor. . . . You commit the great blasphemy against all doctrine and you begin to live' (p. 47). As Conrad's choice of example suggests he and Rosa are still inhabiting a world structured around the opposed terms of racist language. When Rosa ends her relationship with Conrad she does so in terms which suggest important connections with Lionel and Baasie:

> I left the children's tree-house we were living in, in an intimacy of self-engrossment without the reserve of adult accountability, accepting each other's encroachments as the law of the litter, treating each other's dirt as our own, as little Baasie and I had long ago performed the child's black mass, tasting on a finger the gall of our own shit and the saline of our own pee. . . . And you know we had stopped making love together months before I left, aware that it had become incest. (p. 70)

Rosa recoils from Conrad's erotic activities, which depend upon the replacement of the father, because these activities are perceived as dirty and incestuous. The closer Conrad comes to Rosa, the more he blasphemes against her family's beliefs, the more he approaches Baasie, the black 'brother' with whom her first 'dirty' acts were committed. For Rosa sexual freedom is forever connected to images of the black, and to imperfectly suppressed incestuous desires. Significantly Conrad later sails off upon a yacht to islands in the Indian Ocean. Rosa departs for Paris, an unreal place, 'Paris – a place far away in England' (p. 56) as she describes it as a child, and thence to the South of France, to the arms of a surrogate mother, Lionel's first wife, who placed erotic freedom before the needs of the party.

Rosa's arrival in the South of France is described in terms which establish it as the enchanted land of fantasy. 'The silk tent of morning sea' (p. 214) tilts below her plane, glimpsed through the distorting glass of the window. Below, tables outside a bar become 'tiny islands' in 'a day without landmarks'. On the verge 'roadside tapestry flowers grow' and in the background 'a child's pop-up picture book castle' (p. 217) stands against a landscape of sea and flowers. Rosa's perceptions are dazed here, as if entering a dream world, a world drowning in sensuality. Katya's dining room appears as 'swimming colours, fronds blobbing out of focus and a sea horizon undulating in uneven panes of glass' (p. 220). Katya's reminiscences of the party – vodka, parties, sexual affairs – accompany Rosa's meal while she is 'dissolving' (p. 222) in the pleasures of wine, and French sights, sounds, and tastes. A room has been prepared for Rosa at the top of the house, full of feminine bric-a-brac, flowers, mirrors, peaches:

> a room made ready for someone imagined. A girl, a creature whose sense of existence would be in her nose buried in flowers, peach juice running down her chin, face tended at mirrors, mind dreamily averted, body seeking pleasure. Rosa Burger entered, going forward into possession by that image. (pp. 229–30)

Rosa is thus presented with an image of herself as sensual woman, created by Katya, an image which she delightedly assumes, enjoying the sensual pleasures of an unreal country where her projections are reflected back to her, where she ceases to be her father's daughter and becomes instead the mistress of Bernard Chabalier. The particular features of the landscape – islands, tapestry, flowers, mirrors, silk tent – are focused in the tapestry series 'La Dame à la Licorne' which is presented to the reader after Rosa's return to Africa.

Rosa's lover plans to show her these tapestries. He also takes her to see an exhibition of paintings by Bonnard. As he says, 'In Africa, one goes to see the people. In Europe it's paintings' (p. 286). The white in Africa sees people as objects to be contemplated, objects which mirror his own projections. In Europe art offers a timeless substitute reality. Bernard points out that Bonnard's style and subjects never changed. The woman painted in 1894, the mimosa painted in 1945 are treated in the same way. In the fifty years between the paintings there was the growth of fascism, two wars, the Occupation, but for Bonnard it is as if nothing has happened. The two paintings could have been executed on the same day. The woman's flesh and the leaves around her are equal manifestations: 'Because she hasn't any existence any more than the leaves have, outside this lovely forest where they are. . . . Your forest girl and the vase of mimosa – C'est un paradis inventé' (p. 287). With Bernard Rosa lives in a similar invented paradise, a world of sensual pleasures, divorced from historical events, a world in which she is only a timeless image. Rosa meets Bernard for the first time in a mirrored bar which suggests the solipsism of France for her. 'In the bar where she had sat seeing others living in the mirror, there was no threshold between her reflection and herself' (p. 272).

Rosa's rejection of this world is linked to the image presented in the tapestry series. Scholars have suggested various interpretations for the tapestries. A particular focus of difficulty is the sixth tapestry in which the lady, on a blue island, against a rose background strewn with tapestry flowers, stands in front of a silk tent over which hangs the banner motto 'A mon seul désir'. The lady appears to be taking a necklace from a box and the tapestry has thus been understood as celebrating a gift of love. Gordimer draws upon the most recent scholarly explanation. In the text she describes the first tapestry, the lady holding a mirror in which the unicorn is reflected, and then simply lists the four following tapestries as 'the representation of the other four senses' (p. 340), hearing, smell, taste, touch. The text then moves to the sixth tapestry which is discussed in more detail. In 1978 Alain Erlande-Brandenburg[38] agreed that the tapestries represent the five senses, but suggested that the meaning of the sixth tapestry lay not in the acceptance of a gift but rather in its renunciation: the lady is not receiving the necklace but replacing it in the box. The sixth tapestry may therefore be understood as signifying the need not to submit to the power of the senses but to exercise free will in their control. The necklace therefore symbolizes the renunciation of the passions which may interfere with our ability to act morally. 'A mon seul désir' translates as 'by my own free will'. Where formerly the tapestries were understood as celebrating the senses, as embodied in a beautiful woman, the understanding of the sixth panel has now corrected the eye of the observer.

On the simplest level, therefore, the tapestries indicate that Rosa's decision to abandon the sensual joys of life with her lover is an act of free will, a renunciation of the fantasy eroticism of projection, mirror images, and magic islands. Life with Bernard would remove her from her historical destiny, to a 'place' outside time. Gordimer's description of the tapestries is entirely in the present tense, a timeless participial present which creates an impression of enchanted stillness. 'The Lion and the Unicorn listening to music. . . . The Lady weaving. . . . The Lady taking sweets from a dish . . .' (p. 340). In France Rosa has been possessed by an image of herself as sensual, floating like the lady on 'an azure island of a thousand flowers' (p. 340), hearing nightingales sing, delighting in the taste of French foods and the sights of France, enjoying the touch of a lover. For all their beauty, however, the tapestries were executed in 'the age of the thumbscrew and dungeon' (p. 341). Bernard would take Rosa away from a similar world of pain and imprisonment in order to sequester her in a private world of sensual joy and art, a world in which he could show her the tapestries he loves: 'to love you by letting you come to discover what I love' (p. 341). What Bernard loves is an image of Rosa to which she does not entirely correspond. In the extremely complex presentation of the tapestries Gordimer describes a woman gazing at them, a woman who has all the time in the

82

world to do so. 'There she sits gazing, gazing. And if it is time for the museum to close, she can come back tomorrow and another day, any day, days. Sits gazing, this creature that has never been' (p. 341). In the 'Sight' tapestry the lady is also gazing, into a hand-held mirror, but she sees only the reflection of the unicorn, the mythical creature which has never existed outside the human mind. Rosa Burger may become, like the lady, a gazer into a hand-held mirror which reflects back to her only an unreal and mythical creature, a woman who has only existed in the projections of others. In returning to South Africa, however, Rosa chooses not to be such an image, an object to be displayed and desired, a figure in an erotic or political iconography. In South Africa Rosa acquired a false identity imposed upon her by others. Pursuing a personal erotic course, however, simply creates an alternative mask. Rosa's progress towards autonomy involves coming to terms with the mythic masks which men have fastened over the female face – whether desexualized or erotically reified – and correcting the errors of her own internal eye.

Where the tapestry series articulates the necessity of correcting the errors of the eye, Baasie's voice establishes the autonomous existence of 'You'. Rosa wakes in the night to 'the telephone ringing buried in the flesh' (p. 318) and in the darkness at first assumes it is her lover. When she realizes it is Baasie she tries to put him off. When Baasie keeps telling Rosa to put on the light Rosa refuses on the grounds that it is late; she will see him 'tomorrow – today, I suppose it is, it's still so dark' (p. 319). Rosa would very much like to keep this conversation in a timeless darkness. To her Baasie is not a person with an autonomous existence, but a creature of her own mind: 'The way you look in my mind is the way my brother does – never gets any older' (p. 323). She addresses him as Baasie. The childish nickname infantilizes and desexualizes an adult male, converting him into a 'boy'. For Rosa his real name, Zwelinzima Vulindlela, is unknown and unpronounceable. In response Baasie insists angrily that he is not her 'black brother' (p. 321) and doesn't have 'to live in your head' (p. 323). He will not enter into a relationship with her in which he functions as a psychological surrogate. His insults force Rosa to put on the light, and externalize his voice, no longer a part of Rosa, but a person in his own right, challenging her. By taunting her, 'he had disposed of her whining to go back to bed and bury them both' (p. 322). Burying the body is a part of Rosa's strategy, as it is Clare Terblanche's. She, too, would like to live in a world which corresponds to childish projections, in which the magical landscape is more real than a 'Suffering Land' (Zwelinzima). In the conversation Baasie can only be 'You', a voice without pronounceable identity. Up to this point in the novel Rosa may be said to have addressed a 'You' of fantasy. Now, however, 'You' answers back. At the end of the conversation, vomiting in front of the bathroom mirror, Rosa sees herself as 'Ugly, soiled' (p. 324), 'filthy' and 'debauched'. She comments, 'how I disfigured myself' (p. 329). Disfiguration is an essential step in Rosa's progress towards autonomy, an autonomy which depends upon confrontation with her real body, repugnant as well as beautiful, a body which cannot be split into good, clean white, or bad, dirty, black.

Rosa returns to South Africa to take up her father's work in two senses: first in terms of a renewed political commitment, and second in the tending of black bodies. As a physiotherapist, Rosa (like her doctor father) restores feelings to the nerves of injured black people. Rosa's return is to a world of repugnant bodies, horribly mutilated in the Soweto riots, but she is now able to face these bodies and act in their world. When Rosa is charged with abetting the schoolchildren's revolt the reader has no external evidence for the truth of the accusation. Internally, however, Rosa had participated in a schoolgirl's revolt against paternalism, a revolt which has brought her to political consciousness. The novel ends with a revolt against parents which is not the product of white fantasy, but a political and historical reality. The schoolchildren's revolt in Soweto is directed at the white paternalist state, but also at the political compromises of black fathers. Fats Mxenge is such a

father, a man who appears at the end of the novel like 'someone
brought aboard out of a tempest' (p. 343).

JULY'S PEOPLE

A postscript remains: *July's People* in which the focus shifts
from psychological to economic determinants. In 'Apprentices
of Freedom', an essay drawing its title from Mannoni, Gordimer stated her belief that 'racial problems, both material and
spiritual, can hope to be solved only in circumstances of equal
economic opportunity.'[39] As *July's People* opens, Maureen
Smales, a refugee from war-torn Johannesburg, awakens with
her children and husband, Bam, in the rural village of her
servant, July, still lurching to the motion of their three-day
journey to safety in their bakkie: 'as the swell of the sea makes
the land heave under-foot when the passenger steps ashore
after a voyage' (p. 3). Although Maureen, like Fats Mxenge,
appears to have reached safe harbour in the bakkie, 'a ship that
had docked in a far country' (p. 14), in fact her voyage has only
just begun. Marooned in July's village, this particular Miranda
has yet to discover the full horror of a cultural shipwreck
involving the collapse of stable identities together with the loss
of all her values and certainties, as dreams of escape turn into
nightmare. 'People in delirium rise and sink, rise and sink, in
and out of lucidity. . . . The vehicle was the fever. Chattering
metal and raving dance of loose bolts' (p. 3). Gordimer has
described the force of revolutionary change in South Africa as a
'demonic dance'.[40] In *July's People* the rhythm of the voyage
transmutes into that of social change as songs, the sound of the
cowhide drum, chants, radio music, a 'gumba-gumba' (bat-
tery-operated record player) provide an escalating background
which culminates when ex-dancer Maureen ('Under-10s Silver
Cup for Classical and Mime': p. 2) perceives a change in the
surrounding fabric of sounds, 'breaks into another rhythm' (p.
159) and runs to the 'beat' (p. 160) of a 'dervish' (p. 159)
helicopter, dancing out of the pages of the novel towards an
uncertain future.

85

In the intervening period the delusions of the Liberal Smales are stripped away to reveal the economic bases of their existence. Maureen's evolving relationship with July, a reworking of Rosa's with Baasie, dramatizes Gordimer's concern as to whether people can 'make a common culture if their material interests conflict dramatically'.[41] In this liminal interregnum between the Republic of South Africa and 'Azania' Maureen comes to realize that the traits which she had admired in her Man Friday were not his essential character, but merely assumed in order to conform to her mental image of him. As July's mask slips, 'an explosion of roles' (p. 117) ensues. July, always apparently honest, turns out to have filched small household articles (rediscovered in the village), confronting Maureen with the realization that 'honesty is how much you know about anybody' (p. 36). If Maureen knows little of July, not even his real name, Mwawate, she is equally deficient in self-knowledge. Out of 'necessity' (p. 38) she also steals (malaria pills). Out of the need for meat, Bam becomes a killer (of warthogs). The horrible possibility dawns on the Smales that their fine moral values are context-bound, dependent upon the means available. The point is expanded in relation to sexual morality. The Smales comprehend the 'rights of sexual love as formulated in master bedrooms' (p. 65) as opposed to the very different formulations of a wife's hut, or a servant's back room. July has been forced by his two-year migratory labour pattern to strike a balance between duty and desire, based on 'the lovers' place in the economy' (p. 65), providing economically for his wife Martha while enjoying a mistress, Ellen, in town. Once deprived of the privacy of the master bedroom, crammed onto car seats in a mud hut in close proximity to their children, the Smales undergo an almost complete loss of desire. In *this* revolution, sexual intimacy is not so much rearranged as annulled. In contrast to Rosa's fantasy world, the 'fairy ring' (p. 26) village continually outrages the senses, as Maureen smells the sour odour of unwashed bodies, menstruates in rags, is pursued for her excrement by pigs, and sidesteps insects, vomit, and fowl-droppings. On the one occasion of lovemaking, sexuality becomes horror, when Bam, seeing his wife's menstrual blood on his penis, thinks for a hallucinatory moment that it is the blood of the dead pig (p. 80). Imagistically it is: the couple only make love because excited by gorging on warthog. The quasi-castration image also underlines the extent to which, divested of the attributes of male power (bakkie and weapon, both commandeered by blacks) Bam is progressively desexualized. Maureen, undepilated, weather-beaten, her blonde streaks growing out, undergoes a similar evolution, reminding Bam forcibly of her father. Even her nudity becomes asexual, her bared breasts 'a castration of his sexuality and hers' (p. 90). The implication, that the Smales' new economic condition regulates their sexuality, crystallizes as July replaces Bam as provider and guarantor, and Maureen focuses increasingly on him to fulfil all her wants. In the deconstruction of their previous socially-ordained gender roles Maureen's idleness (she abandons all pretence of childcare) is only an exaggeration of her former function in society, trading sexuality for economic security, not working but living off black labour (in broad terms) and male labour (in the specific examples of Bam and July).

Both thematically and stylistically Gordimer draws attention to the ambiguity of meanings divorced from their context of means.[42] July's initial appearance with morning tea, normal in Johannesburg, becomes grotesque in the context of a mud hut, as grotesque as his ritual offering of fresh fruit to end a meal of porridge and wild spinach. As the Smales' 'host' (p. 1) he ministers to ambiguous guests-cum-parasites. The implicit question of the title (Who are July's people? The Smales, the villagers, neither?) turns upon a defining context of possession and dispossession. Where Maureen's mother distinguished between her servant ('Our Jim') and her husband ('My Jim') by different possessives, Maureen, now dependent on July, begins to elide the two roles. As identities collapse, pronominal distinctions follow suit. Only context supplies a meaning to the reader who frequently has to backtrack from 'him' or 'them' to identify unspecified referents. Thus, when Maureen thinks

'Always a moody bastard. . . . She had indulged him, back there. She had been afraid – to lose him, the comforts he provided' (p. 64) the reader realizes only sequentially that she is referring not to Bam, back there in Johannesburg, but to July in a preceding scene. Bam has become 'someone recollected' (p. 93) just as Maureen ceases to be recognizable as 'his wife' and becomes only 'Her' (p. 105). In conversation the couple never need to specify 'him' as July. In the context of their total dependence 'there was no one else' (p. 154).

Inevitably as changes in economic status transform the culturally inscribed values of language, so literature itself comes into question. Attempting to read *I Promessi Sposi* Maureen finds that

> the transport of a novel, the false awareness of being within another time, place and life . . . was not possible. . . . No fiction could compete with what she was finding she did not know, could not have imagined or discovered through imagination. They had nothing. (p. 29)

Though the last sentence applies primarily to the material poverty of the villagers, the moral and cultural bankruptcy of the Smales is also implicated. Later, Maureen finds that the novel, an English translation, 'would not translate from the page to the kind of comprehension she was able to provide now' (p. 138). In her hungry nostalgia only an account of bread riots holds its meaning. At its broadest the experience suggests the potential limitations of imaginative fiction, the product of a certain level of privacy, leisure, and education. In the extreme context of the South African situation, the values of Eurocentric fiction risk transformation into abstractions, belied by concrete economic realities. More specifically *July's People* foregrounds the problematic relation between narrative and cultural authority. The only other books in the village, July's pass-book, post-office book, and savings book, are equally outdated. In the past, July regarded his money as safe, 'written down in those books' just as his identity was guaranteed by the Smales' signatures. Now the books are 'just bits of paper' (p. 136). Previously the villagers were able 'to make the connection between the abstract and the concrete', between money and the 'things that bits of paper could be transformed into' (p. 28). Now, as the economic base crumbles, so other abstractions (honesty, dignity, fidelity) disappear, a cultural currency now devalued. Structurally Gordimer implicitly signals the need to cede interpretive control, to deconstruct the authority of the white 'teller' in economic and literary terms. As Greenstein has noted, Gordimer neither ignores July's story, nor presumes to tell it; it remains inaccessible to the white imagination.[43]

Between Maureen and Bam the battle for interpretive control concentrates upon the past. Recriminations fly, Maureen denouncing Bam's 'rearrangement of facts' (p. 46), Bam accusing Maureen of overdramatizing, preparing a 'story' (p. 47) to sell to the papers. In the present the couple focus upon their radio, the last link with their world. Reception is poor, broadcasts infrequent, the reassuring news possibly a 'Bunker fantasy' (p. 88) from a temporary hideout. Lacking any African languages (reduced with the villagers to scraps of Afrikaans, the language of the oppressor) the Smales are exceptionally poor interpreters of their immediate world. Maureen, who prides herself on her ability to name the local flora in Latin, cannot tell poisonous plants from spinach; Bam cannot distinguish the local chief from his headman. Indeed, in audience with the chief, the Smales are inattentive, struggling instead to interpret a recent broadcast in Portuguese. Throughout the novel Maureen always assumes that any utterance is directed at her, that she is 'the one addressed' (p. 117), that it is for her to interpret and mediate. At the chief's, however, July becomes the interpreter; the Smales are the subject of his narration, as their story is rehearsed and interpreted in terms of other cultural assumptions. When the chief assigns Bam a new role (weapons instructor) the Smales are aghast to realize that their imagined liberation struggle is envisaged by the chief, less as a race war than as an intertribal conflict. Unable to explain his position, Bam recognizes that he needs 'words that were not phrases from back there, words that would make the truth that must be forming here' (p. 127), but that the words are blocked by an older white vocabulary ('rural backwardness', 'counter-revolutionary pockets') incomprehensible to the chief.

In contrast to Bam, July's English lacks all abstractions and any tense but the present. A series of confrontations, rising in verbal violence, between July and Maureen, expose Maureen's desire to translate July into her own cultural terms, to interpret their relationship in ways flattering to her own self-image. 'Who tells whom?' is the key emphasis in each scene. Maureen's threat to tell tales on July to Martha (about Ellen) evokes the response: 'What you can tell? That I'm work for you fifteen years. That you satisfy with me' (p. 98). In addition to the bald statement that Maureen can tell nothing of July, outside their economic relation, the sexual double-entendre ('you satisfy') counters the threat by associating Maureen, July's economic 'mistress' in town, with his 'town woman' (p. 16), Ellen. The three senses of tell (telling on, telling a story, telling as command) are indistinguishable to July, in whose semantics betrayal, interpretation on others' cultural terms, and authority are equivalent. In the past Maureen had supplied July's tenses, adopting a simple vocabulary: 'They could assume comprehension between them only if she kept away from even the most commonplace of abstractions' (p. 96). Now she realizes that interpretive control has passed to July; his tense is hers. 'The present was his; he would arrange the past to suit it' (p. 96). Previously when uncertain of his meaning, Maureen relied on a non-committal response, waiting 'to read back his meaning from the context of what he said next' (p. 97). In their new economic context, however, her understanding founders, together with her distinctions between abstract and concrete. When July tells her not to work for his women 'in their place' (p. 97) she cannot know whether to translate as 'instead of them', or as a claim to a specific territory, an indication of her own dispossession. Importantly her uncertainty is also the reader's. Throughout the novel the meanings of African words are made clear by their context (e.g. umlungu, nkosi, morema, hosi (p. 117)/'white boss'; nhwanyana (p. 131)/'my lady'). But when Bam, in search of the stolen gun, questions the villagers, the words 'Mi ta twa ku nandziha ngopfu, swi famba a moyeni. Ncino wa maguva lawa, hey − i . . . hey − i!' (p. 141) are neither translated to Bam or the reader. Only a literate Tsonga/ Shangaan speaker will appreciate the ironic reference to the image of the dance in the novel.[44] Similarly in the culminating scene with July, when the latter bursts out at Maureen in his own language, no translation follows. Nonetheless, 'She understood although she knew no word. Understood everything: what he had had to be, how she had covered up to herself for him, in order for him to be her idea of him' (p. 152). At last Maureen recognizes that her values, her standards of interpretation are irrelevant: 'his measure as a man was taken elsewhere' (p. 156). The gulf between them is emphasized as Maureen adopts a provocative pose on the bakkie, a parody of her own sexual and economic dependency, as unreadable to July as his rhetoric is to her. Maureen never informs Bam that Daniel has the gun. 'Telling' in all its senses is at an end for her.

If the novel ends in characteristically open fashion, the manner of its closure nevertheless highlights the end of Maureen's illusions. Importantly the helicopter's effect on her is registered in sexual terms, as a vibration filling her body, 'a force pumping, jigging in its monstrous orgasm' (p. 158). As its landing-gear descends 'like spread legs' from its 'belly', the 'rutting racket' attracts Maureen into the bush. Though a vine gives off a smell of boiled potatoes, promising 'a kitchen, a house' (p. 160), though clumps of daisies recall a public park, it is clear that Maureen's previous accommodations of Africa to her own concepts of domesticity and order are now placed as delusory: 'The real fantasies of the bush delude more inventively than the romantic forests of Grimm and Disney' (p. 160). Initially Maureen had envisaged her escape as a miracle, casting July as 'frog prince, saviour' (p. 9). Now consoling European fairy-tales are at an end. The unmarked helicopter may contain 'saviours or murderers' (p. 158), black guerrillas or white mercenaries, but Maureen's story will be defined by other conventions, and will make sense only in the context of an unimaginable future.

5

CONCLUSION

A SPORT OF NATURE

Conclusions, even interim conclusions, which merely restate and summarize preceding arguments can be tiresome to both reader and writer. Fortunately in this case we can end on a new beginning, Gordimer's latest novel, *A Sport of Nature*, published just as this study reached completion. Set against a background which embraces most of Africa and extends in time from the 1950s to an independent black South Africa in the near future, the novel returns to many of Gordimer's key concerns. As a *Bildungsroman* it shares its form with *The Lying Days*, *A World of Strangers*, and *Burger's Daughter*; as a chilling dissection of the South African bourgeoisie and a vigorous repudiation of reformist liberalism, it recalls *Occasion for Loving* and *The Late Bourgeois World*. A mythic subtext offers obvious connections to *The Conservationist*, while the futuristic ending provides a counter-example to the apocalyptic vision of *July's People*. As in *A Guest of Honour*, African nationalist politics are a major focus, with the emphasis falling once more upon sexuality as innately radical. If the exploration of love, particularly family love, as a microcosm of political attachments, takes the reader into familiar territory, the picaresque mode of the novel represents a new departure.

As Greenstein has noted,[45] the white woman has always tended to be marginalized in the literature of imperialism. Fictional treatments of colonialism feature male 'adventurers', with the daughters of Empire firmly relegated to a subordinate role. From the beginning of her career Gordimer has proceeded from a recognition of the complex interaction of gender with genre, so that it is no surprise to discover that her latest novel provides a welcome corrective to literary and political readings of Empire which concentrate exclusively on the male hero. *A Sport of Nature* focuses on a female 'adventuress', rewriting the meaning of the term to include sexuality within a positive hypothesis.

Hillela, the heroine of the novel, is described by its title as a *lusus naturae*: 'a plant, animal, etc., which exhibits abnormal variation or a departure from the parental stock.' (*OED*). A spontaneous mutation, Hillela enters the novel as the child of an adulterous mother, Ruth, who departs for Mozambique and a Portuguese lover, abandoning her daughter to the care of her two sisters, first Olga, arch-bourgeois representative of a sterile world of expensive *objets d'art*, then Pauline, who is progressively embittered by her exclusion from the black world in which she formerly exercised her liberal conscience. Expelled from school in Rhodesia for consorting with a 'coloured' boy, Hillela returns to South Africa only to outrage her adoptive family's norms by a quasi-incestuous affair with her cousin/adoptive brother, Sasha. Rejected by both sisters, this latter-day Cinderella embarks on a series of adventures, appearing successively as a go-go dancer, the lover of a duplicitous white journalist, a beach bum in East Africa, the mistress of a Belgian diplomat (Tanzania, an unspecified French-speaking, African country, Accra), the wife of a black South African freedom-fighter (assassinated in Ghana), and thence via Eastern Europe and an aid-related career in America to return to South Africa for its independence celebrations as the wife of the President of the OAU, General Reuel.

The narrative technique of the novel is highly unusual. Throughout, Hillela is viewed almost entirely from an external point of view. The narrator pieces together her history as if researching the biography of a public figure, admitting lacunae in the account, speculating as to motive, and tracking an evanescent subject through multiple changes of identity. Named in honour of a Zionist great-grandfather, Hillela shucks off her awkward forename to assume the protective colonial colouration of 'Kim', amidst the Susans, Clares, and Fionas of her Rhodesian school. Reverting in South Africa to Hillela Capran, she is later transmogrified into Mrs Whaila Kgomani, and finally rebaptised Chiemeka (Igbo: God has done very well) by her second husband. Various historical figures enjoy walk-on parts (Oliver Tambo, Tennyson Maki-wane, Joshua Nkomo, Archbishop Tutu) as does the fictional Rosa Burger. It is tempting to perceive this narrative technique as consciously Marxist, as Hillela changes according to the forces of circumstances and history. The external perspective certainly registers the crisis of the Liberal view of the individual subject, with its accompanying assumptions of the organic coherence of the individual, transcending social conditions. On the other hand, as the narrator remarks, the gaps and silences in the life-story also associate Hillela, via similar lacunae, with the lives of individual heroes: 'In the lives of the greatest, there are such lacunae – Christ and Shakespeare disappear from and then reappear in the chronicles that documentation and human memory provide' (p. 270). Indeed, her mysterious paternity, early abandonment, surrogate parents, expulsion as taboo-breaker, exile, wanderings, trials, and triumphal return all link Hillela with the paradigm of the mythical (male) hero, as delineated by Lord Raglan (*The Hero*, 1936). A strong myth-ical undertow runs as a subtext to the novel which pullulates with references to Greek tragedy, myth, folk- and fairy-tales.

Although Gordimer employs Hillela to rewrite a male-centred myth, recasting a familiar western paradigm in female terms, myth should not be confused with apolitical mystifica-tion. In interview, Gordimer recalled that on their release from jail after Soweto black writers sparked off a resurgence of interest in black heroes of the past (Chaka or Dingaan, for example) who answered 'a need for myths which fed fervour' (*Observer*, 29 March 1987, p. 21). If the futuristic conclusion to the novel appears somewhat Utopian, it is possible that this is deliberate strategy on Gordimer's part – to compose an ending to encourage just such an ending to the present Republic of South Africa. As Sasha comments: 'Utopia is unattainable; without aiming for it . . . you can never hope even to fall far short of it' (p. 217). Reuel's African name (also 'God has done very well') is etymologically Utopian, given for 'what the name will make happen' (p. 308). Hillela names her daughter Nomzamo (after Winnie Mandela) though the choice backfires into irony when Nomzamo rechristens herself Nomo to become a model. Throughout the novel Gordimer provides both occasions for fervour, and for irony, in the recognition that irony is the price of aiming high. The reportorial voice of the narrator, laboriously reconstructing past events, lends the novel a mock-historical tone, implying that only time will tell whether 'mock' or 'historical' should be the key emphasis. Hillela's own elusive status thus offers the reader a choice of potential stories – that of a quasi-mythical revolutionary heroine, or (in the ironic reading) that of a sexual adventuress, at best the passive handmaiden of revolution. Similarly the naive, childish quality of Hillela's political illusions appears to be highlighted in frequent fairy tale motifs – Hillela as Sleeping Beauty (p. 162), as Cinderella rising from rags to riches via a succession of princes (p. 186), diverted from the ANC guerrilla camp at Bagamoyo to visit an 'Arabian Nights' (p. 172) hotel, gigglingly comparing the discovery of incest to the three bears ('Who's been sleeping in *my* bed?': p. 181). The apparent quality of wish-fulfilment in these motifs needs, however, to be set against the background of Soweto, a children's revolt with serious consequences.

In like fashion, the African mythical elements also offer a choice between fervour and irony. At one point Hillela's journalist lover cross-questions a group of activists about Qamata, described as 'a sort of church' (p. 137):

He comes from the sea –
  – One of our gods, Xhosa gods . . .
  – I was told he was the 'ruler of the spirits.' . . . But is the

idea that Qamata . . . an African god, a Xhosa god is something that can chase away the god of submission, the Christian god who says 'thou shalt not kill', and make killing a sacrifice for freedom? (pp. 137–8)

Qamata, the Xhosa Supreme Being, may have originated in the name of an epic hero, credited with supernatural powers,[46] but has been associated in modern times with the revolts in the Transkei of the late 1950s and early 1960s, which gave rise to the 'Poqo' campaign. Poqo (Xhosa 'alone') was the name adopted by one of the largest black clandestine organizations of the 1960s, to distinguish it from other, multiracial movements. In November 1967, one Poqo activist testified in court that in 1961 he had joined Poqo and its 'sort of church Qamata'. Quasi-religious oathings were reported at the time and some whites inevitably regarded Poqo as akin to Mau Mau. Though the precise role of Qamata remains obscure,[47] it indicates the potential power of mythical symbols to be carriers of political change. In drawing attention to Qamata as emerging from the sea, however, Gordimer awakens echoes of an earlier Xhosa revolt, which place the power of myth in a less affirmative perspective. In the early nineteenth century the coming of the whites put pressure on the Xhosa who resisted violently and also sought to tap new sources of power through 'prophets' (e.g. Nxele) who foretold a mass resurrection of the ancestors, in which the dead would rise from their graves in the sea to drive out the whites. Sightings of past heroes emerging from the sea in battle array culminated in the 'national suicide' of the Xhosa, who slaughtered their cattle to propitiate the ancestors and, when millennium failed, turned upon each other.

In *A Sport of Nature* Gordimer exploits both positive and negative readings of the power of myth. Whaila Kgomani is repeatedly described as godlike, 'the disguised god from the sea' (p. 231), 'the obsidian god from the waves' (p. 251) and first meets Hillela in the sea at Tamarisk Beach, his 'water-smoothed head of antiquity' (p. 164) appearing from the waves

97

to bring news of an assassination to Arnold, the commander in exile. On his arrival 'siren' (p. 164) Hillela simply turns tail, leaving the men as 'the navigators of the world's courses' (p. 164). Later, marriage to Whaila appears to convert Hillela from 'jetsam' (p. 163) to purpose, but ironies also surface. In Ghana the couple enjoy Sundays at the beach, enclosed in 'A perfect circle of sand', to quote the chapter title. Arriving on one occasion to find their beach a declared cholera area, they make an excursion to Tema, Nkrumah's deep-sea harbour, described as holding 'half-circled the power of the sea' (p. 225). Surveying this evidence of the emergent strength of black nationalism Whaila seems godlike, 'as if dusted with gold' (p. 225). Yet Nkrumah has already fallen from power, an 'Osagyefo' (leader) whose people virtually declared him a god only to destroy him. Hillela realizes that the power on which Whaila rides is fundamentally unstable:

> she suddenly understood fear . . . in the huge upheaval which she had placed herself astride as when a child she had revelled in the wild bucking of a playground's mythical bull. Another had risen, out of the sea, Zeus disguised to capture Europa . . . and carried her off, clinging to its legendary black back. (p. 223)

An equally ominous note is struck when the couple end the day with a visit to the grave of another black hero, Du Bois, whom Whaila quotes: 'I saw the face of freedom . . . and I died' (p. 226).

After Whaila's death, Hillela, as a tragic widow with a black child, becomes an 'ikon' (p. 321) of reconciliation between the Third World and the West, an image of reform rather than revolution. In Eastern Europe the 'mythical wooden beasts' (p. 265) of the children's playground are furred with snow, the only hero (Karel) aged and bypassed by events. Sensually Hillela appears to be frozen, until her encounter with Reuel, which has the effect of resexualization and repoliticization. Significantly the couple come together after an accident in which their car skids, wrenching Hillela off course 'as if on the stirrup of a bucking monster' (p. 315). Returning to the sea in Mombasa, Hillela reflects

> Lusaka was landlocked, Eastern Europe and the brown-stone locked each year in snow. . . . She floated and recalled without pain . . . the emergence of the obsidian arms, head and torso from this sea. The water itself washed pain away; there was only the sensuality with which it did. (p. 318)

Sensually reawakened, Hillela recommits herself to the violent African struggle, which culminates in the Independence celebrations at which the masses appear 'as if the ocean itself has flooded up from Table Bay' (p. 393).

The implicit connection between sensuality and activism is also related to the Utopian theme. Sasha continued his reflections in the following terms:

> Instinct is utopian. Emotion is utopian. . . . Without utopia – the idea of utopia – there's a failure of the imagination – and that's a failure to go on living. It will take another kind of being to stay on, here. A new white person. Not us. The chance is a wild chance – like falling in love. (p. 218)

In interview[48] Gordimer drew attention to the confluence of political and sexual radicalism in the novel. Though apparently growing into militancy through the force of historical circumstances, Hillela remains unconditioned by the family and outside the cultural norms of her native land, recreating herself at every turn to slough off successive lives and move on. Her self-creation proceeds on grounds of instinct rather than ideology; her personality is of itself so luxuriant as to eclipse the attractions of material luxury (*Observer* intervew). In the midst of the cruelty that is South Africa, individual love appears as selfish, while 'brotherly love' becomes an idea beset by sophistry, as Hillela's lovemaking with her 'brother' demonstrates to her ostensibly Liberal family. Only sexual love remains as a touchstone of integrity, whether personal or political. In South Africa the laws that govern African lives are based on the body (skin colour, relative thickness of lips: p. 206) and therefore have to be fought through the body. If there is a driving force which transforms Hillela's picaresque adventures into a purposive quest it is the desire to follow her instinctive need for an erotic relation, and a family, of a radically different type. By the accident of her early abandonment, Hillela becomes an exile from childhood, an eternal guest of honour, going 'home' in school holidays to a family location chosen arbitrarily for her by others. The abstract relations of her childhood free her from 'patricidal and infanticidal loves between parents and children' (p. 332). Knowing her mother only as a sexual being, through a discovered cache of explicit love-letters, she avoids the 'Calvinism and koshering' (p. 59) of her mother's background. Accustomed to displacement, she readily learns to move to successive postings for political reasons. For Hillela, 'without a cause is without a home' (p. 189). Importantly when she at last rediscovers her mother she makes no attempt to reclaim the abandoned relationship, or to discover the true identity of her father, having relocated herself within the family of a cause (p. 245). The central event of her youth, perceived by her aunts as a definitive breach of the taboos of the bourgeois family, is quite simply not incest at all for unrepressed Hillela. An emblematic act, it provides a proleptic image of 'children with the house to themselves' (p. 95) in a future state of independence. It also poses the question of the relation between brotherhood and love. Pauline, theoretically a believer in brotherhood, promptly expels Hillela from the bosom of the family. Hillela's emergent sexuality thus strips the family of its illusions, making the point that there can be no family life for whites when blacks are denied it, that Hillela cannot 'set up home again in the house where only white people could live' (p. 159). Instead Whaila becomes 'lover and brother to her in the great family of a cause' (p. 250). Whaila understands imperialism in familial terms, as originating in the interrelated monarchies of the nineteenth century ('all the same family weren't they? Cousins, uncles') then with foreign national economies forming 'the extended family of the West' (p. 202). Hillela's evolution runs in parallel as she moves,

100

less from lover to lover, than through a succession of families, as surrogate daughter and lover to the Belgian ambassador, to whose children she is nanny, 'cousin' (p. 185) and 'sister' (p. 192), as hopeful mother of an interracial 'rainbow' family with Whaila, thence to a narrow escape from reintegration into the nuclear model in America, to end up as one of Reuel's three wives, in a non-matrilineal self-invented family paradigm (p. 360) based upon her protection and (it is hinted) seduction of Reuel's son by another wife. Reuel is so free from the exclusive loyalties of family that he has this favourite son kidnapped (and worse) for political ends. Hillela's own pride in Nomzamo depends precisely on a reversal of the usual parental feeling, a delight in *not* having reproduced herself all over again in another privileged white child (p. 228). In Hillela's view exclusive, individual love 'can't be got away with' (p. 269). It is envisaged as fostering bourgeois counter-revolution in eastern Europe (p. 267), quietism in America. For Hillela, the heir to the Reichian understanding of *A Guest of Honour*, the only love that counts is owed to the 'hungry crowds' (p. 269). Her commitment to the extended family of African nationalism develops from a clear-eyed, unsentimental perception of the economic reality of the 'rainbow' family:

> The real rainbow family stinks. The dried liquid of dysentery streaks the legs of babies and old men and the women smell of their monthly blood. They smell of lack of water. They smell of lack of food. They smell of bodies blown up by the expanding gases of their corpses' innards, lying in the bush in the sun. (p. 291)

If Hillela appears eventually to succeed in combining a cause and a home, ironies none the less remain. The implicit connections with a children's revolt of a more specifically political nature, and with the image of whites as child-killers in present-day South Africa, are made explicit in the fate of Sasha, Hillela's male counterpart, who remains caught in the tragic House of Atreus of his South African family. Throughout the novel Sasha has charted the horrors of repressive parents. His pregnant schoolfriend hangs herself, more afraid of parents than of death. Reformist Pauline shelters black Alpheus, but disapproves of his marriage and children. When she discusses the problem with Sasha he comments crisply 'Emasculate him' (p. 72), impatient at adults 'who always knew what the children should do' (p. 73). For all her Liberalism, Pauline's mode of cultural housekeeping maintains the status quo. When Sasha is imprisoned for political activism, he is kept incommunicado apart from permitted visits from his gorgon mother, who succeeds in reasserting the maternal role only via her son's incarceration. While she finds political acceptance once more, founding a committee of detainees' parents and liaising with black parents' committees, for Sasha it is 'like being thrust up back again into the womb' (p. 367). He draws the moral in a letter: 'white kids are being killed in landmine explosions and supermarket bombings, on Sunday rides and shopping trips with their loving parents. The mines and petrol bombs are planted by blacks, but it's the whites who have killed their own children' (p. 373). When the letter is read aloud in the court, it is as much the parents who are on trial as their son. Sasha, despite becoming a hero to blacks, fails to participate in the visionary futurity of the closing pages. Gordimer leaves only time to tell which of the pair, Hillela or Sasha, is the 'sport of nature', which the representative hero. It seems a peculiarly appropriate note on which to end this study.

NOTES

1 Gordimer, 'The prison house of colonialism', *Times Literary Supplement*, 15 August 1980, p. 918.
2 Jannika Hurwitt, 'The art of fiction LXXVII. Nadine Gordimer', *Paris Review*, 88 (1983), p. 89.
3 Clingman, p. 43.
4 See Elizabeth Abel, Marianne Hirsch, and Elizabeth Langland (eds), *The Voyage In: Fictions of Female Development*, Amherst: University Press of New England, 1983.
5 Gordimer, 'Johannesburg', *Holiday*, 18 (1955), pp. 58, 59.
6 Clingman, p. 64.
7 Wade, p. 70. This aspect of the novel has also been elucidated by Cooke, Clingman, and JanMohamed, amongst others.
8 Clingman, p. 82.
9 For a more extensive analysis see Clingman, p. 86.
10 Gordimer, 'Literature and politics in South Africa', *Southern Review*, 7 (1974), p. 214.
11 'Literature and politics', p. 225.
12 Gordimer, 'Modern African writing', *Michigan Quarterly Review*, 9, 4 (1970), p. 229.
13 Ernst Fisher, *The Necessity of Art: A Marxist Approach*, Penguin, 1963. I am grateful for this information to Paul Rich in an unpublished paper (1983) 'Liberal realism in South African fiction, 1948–1966'.
14 Gordimer, 'The essential gesture: writers and responsibility', in Sterling M. McMurrin (ed.), *The Tanner Lectures on Human Values IV*, Cambridge: Cambridge University Press, 1985, p. 8.
15 Abdul R. JanMohamed, *Manichean Aesthetics. The Politics of Literature in Colonial Africa*, Amherst: University of Massachusetts Press, 1983.
16 Jean-Paul Sartre, 'Orphée noir', in L.S. Senghor, *Anthologie de la*

103

nouvelle poésie nègre et malgache de langue française, Paris: Presses Universitaires de France, 1969, pp. ix–xliv.

17 *Rand Daily Mail*, 27 July 1972, p. 4.

18 Philip Rieff, 'The world of Wilhelm Reich', *Commentary*, 38, 3 (1964), p. 51. Rieff's is the most succinct and intelligent commentary on Reich, on which I draw extensively here.

19 Jean Fido, '*A Guest of Honour*: a feminine view of masculinity', *World Literature Written in English*, 17, 1 (1978), pp. 30–7.

20 Honoré de Balzac, *The Girl With The Golden Eyes*, New York: Paperback Library, 1962, pp. 13, 15.

21 Gordimer, 'Censorship and the primary homeland', *Reality*, 1, 6 (1970) pp. 81–3.

22 George Steiner, 'The language animal' (1969), reprinted in *Extraterritorial*, London: Faber, 1972, p. 82.

23 Nadine Gordimer, 'A writer in South Africa', *London Magazine*, 5, 2 (1965).

24 Henry Callaway, *The Religious System of the Amazulu*, London, 1878.

25 The passages quoted occur in Callaway on the following pages: *The Conservationist* pp. 39, 55, Callaway p. 182; *The Conservationist* pp. 77, 87, 107, Callaway p. 194; *The Conservationist* p. 155, Callaway pp. 12–13; *The Conservationist* p. 183, Callaway pp. 134, 136; *The Conservationist* p. 201, Callaway pp. 77–9; *The Conservationist* p. 217, Callaway p. 391; *The Conservationist* p. 233, Callaway, pp. 15–16.

26 Callaway, pp. 3–9.

27 See Axel-Ivar Berglund, *Zulu Thought Patterns and Symbolism*, London: C. Hurst, 1976, pp. 56–8.

28 S.G. Lee, 'Spirit possession among the Zulu', in John Beattie and John Middleton (eds), *Spirit Mediumship and Society in Africa*, London: Routledge & Kegan Paul, 1969, pp. 128–58.

29 Beattie and Middleton, p. xxviii.

30 Berglund, op. cit.

31 Gordimer, 'Literature and politics in South Africa', *Southern Review*, 7, 3 (1974), 205–6.

32 See Ronnie Mutch, 'Growing up with Gordimer', *The Literary Review*, January 1982, 44–5.

33 See Nadine Gordimer, John Dugard, and Richard Smith, *What Happened to Burger's Daughter or How South African Censorship Works*, Emmarentia: Taurus Publications, 1980.

34 Gordon W. Allport, *The Nature of Prejudice*, Cambridge, Mass.: Addison-Wesley, 1954, pp. 376–82.

35 Joel Kovel, *White Racism: A Psychohistory*, London: Penguin, 1970.

36 Octave Mannoni, *Prospero and Caliban: The Psychology of Colonialism*, New York: Praeger, 1956. Gordimer entitled her Neil Gunn Fellowship lecture (1981) 'Apprentices of freedom', quoting the phrase from Mannoni, p. 65.

37 Frantz Fanon, *Black Skin, White Masks*, London: MacGibbon & Kee, 1968, p. 202.

38 Alain Erlande-Brandenburg, *La Dame à la Licorne*, Paris: Editions de la Réunion des Musées Nationaux, 1978.

39 Gordimer, 'Apprentices of freedom', *New Society*, 24/31 December 1981, p. ii.

40 Gordimer, 'Living in the interregnum', *New York Review of Books*, 20 January 1983, p. 21.

41 'Apprentices of freedom', p. ii.

42 See Stephen Clingman, op. cit., and X, 'Fall of a house', *New York Review of Books*, 13 August 1981, pp. 14–18.

43 Susan Greenstein (1985). Nancy Bailey (1984) points out that both July's 'peoples' are dismayed by the reality that replaces their dream fantasies. Martha's story involves a similar disillusion to Maureen's.

44 The language is Tsonga/Shangaan. My informants, T. Mseleku and Mary Bill, both remarked independently that a correct translation depends upon knowledge of the context in which the sentences are spoken. The speaker is addressing the man on the roof, fixing the 'gumba-gumba' apparatus. The sentences translate as 'You will hear how nice it is, travelling through the air. The rhythm/dance of these days/times, hey!', where the final exclamation carries almost a note of disbelief. Given that the Smales are learning only gradually to move to a different cultural rhythm, Bam's incomprehension, together with his assumption that the phrases are addressed to him, is peculiarly appropriate.

45 Susan M. Greenstein, 'Miranda's story: Nadine Gordimer and the literature of Empire', *Novel*, 18, 3 (1985), 227–42.

46 Janet Hodgson, *The God of the Xhosa*, Cape Town: Oxford University Press, 1982.

47 Tom Lodge, 'Izwe-Lethu (The land is ours): Poqo, the politics of despair', in Anne V. Akeroyd and Christopher R. Hill (eds), *Southern African Research in Progress. Collected Papers 3*, University of York: Centre for Southern African Studies, 1978.

48 *Observer*, 29 March 1987, p. 21, which I draw upon extensively in this paragraph.

105

BIBLIOGRAPHY

WORKS BY NADINE GORDIMER

Novels

The Lying Days. London: Gollancz, and New York: Simon & Schuster, 1953.

A World of Strangers. London: Gollancz, and New York: Simon & Schuster, 1958.

Occasion for Loving. London: Gollancz, and New York: Viking Press, 1963.

The Late Bourgeois World. London: Gollancz, and New York: Viking Press, 1966.

A Guest of Honour. New York: Viking Press, 1970; London: Cape, 1971.

The Conservationist. London: Cape, 1974; New York: Viking Press, 1975.

Burger's Daughter. London: Cape, and New York: Viking Press, 1979.

July's People. London: Cape, and New York: Viking Press, 1981.

A Sport of Nature. London: Cape, and New York: Knopf, 1987.

Short stories

Face to Face: Short Stories. Johannesburg: Silver Leaf, 1949.

The Soft Voice of the Serpent and Other Stories. New York: Simon & Schuster, 1952; London: Gollancz, 1953.

Six Feet of the Country. London: Gollancz, and New York: Simon & Schuster, 1956.

Friday's Footprint and Other Stories. London: Gollancz, and New York: Viking Press, 1960.

Not for Publication and Other Stories. London: Gollancz, and New York: Viking Press, 1965.

Penguin Modern Stories 4, with others. London: Penguin, 1970.

Livingstone's Companions. New York: Viking Press, 1971; London: Cape, 1972.

Selected Stories. London: Cape, 1975; New York: Viking Press, 1976; as *No Place Like*, London: Penguin, 1978.

Some Monday for Sure. London: Heinemann, 1976.

A Soldier's Embrace. London: Cape, and New York: Viking Press, 1980.

Town and Country Lovers. Los Angeles: Sylvester & Orphanos, 1980.

Something Out There. London: Cape, and New York: Viking Press, 1984.

Plays

Television Plays and Documentaries: *A Terrible Chemistry* (Writers and Places series, 1981); *Choosing for Justice: Allan Boesak*, with Hugo Cassirer, 1985; *Country Lovers*, *A Chip of Glass Ruby*, *Praise*, and *Oral History* (all in The Gordimer Stories series), 1985.

Other

On the Mines, photographs by David Goldblatt. Cape Town: Struik, 1973.

The Black Interpreters: Notes on African Writing. Johannesburg: Spro-Cas Ravan, 1973.

What Happened to Burger's Daughter; or How South African Censorship Works, with others. Johannesburg: Taurus, 1980.

Editor, with Lionel Abrahams, *South African Writing Today*. London: Penguin, 1967.

Lifetimes: Under Apartheid, photographs by David Goldblatt, London: Cape, 1986.

Bibliography

Robert Green, 'Nadine Gordimer: a bibliography of works and criticism', *Bulletin of Bibliography*, 42, 1, pp. 5–11.

Manuscript Collection: University of Texas, Austin.

Books

Clingman, Stephen R. *The Novels of Nadine Gordimer: History from the Inside*. London: Allen & Unwin, 1986.

Cooke, John. *The Novels of Nadine Gordimer: Private Lives/Public Landscapes*. Baton Rouge: Louisiana State University Press, 1985.

Haugh, Robert F. *Nadine Gordimer*. New York: Twayne, 1974.

Heywood, Christopher. *Nadine Gordimer*. Windsor, Berks.: Profile, 1983.

JanMohamed, Ahdul R. *Manichean Aesthetics. The Politics of Literature in Colonial Africa*. Amherst: University of Massachusetts Press, 1983.

Nazareth, Peter. *The Third World Writer. His Social Responsibility*. Nairobi: Kenya Literature Bureau, 1978.

Parker, Kenneth. *The South African Novel in English*. London: Macmillan, 1978.

Wade, Michael. *Nadine Gordimer*. London: Evans, 1978.

White, Landeg and Tim Couzens (eds). *Literature and Society in South Africa*. London: Longman, 1984.

Articles

Abrahams, Lionel. 'Nadine Gordimer: the transparent ego', *English Studies in Africa*, 3, 2 (September 1960), 146–51.

Bailey, Nancy. 'Living without the future: Nadine Gordimer's *July's People*', *World Literature Written in English*, 24, 2 (Autumn 1984), 215–24.

Boyers, Robert (ed.). 'Nadine Gordimer: politics and the order of art', *Salmagundi*, LXII (Winter 1984).

Daymond, Margaret. '*Burger's Daughter*: a novel's reliance on history', in M. J. Daymond, J. U. Jacobs and M. Lenta (eds), *Momentum*, Pietermaritzburg: University of Natal Press, 1984.

Driver, Dorothy. 'Nadine Gordimer: the politicisation of women', *English in Africa*, 10, 2 (1983), 29–54.

Fido, Jean. '*A Guest of Honour*: a feminine view of masculinity', *World Literature Written in English*, 17, 1, (1978), 30–7.

Green, Robert. 'Nadine Gordimer's *A World of Strangers*: strains in South African liberalism', *English Studies in Africa*, 22, 1 (March 1979), 45–53.

Green, Robert J. 'Nadine Gordimer's *A Guest of Honour*', *World Literature Written in English*, 16 (1977), 55–66.

Greenstein, Susan M. 'Miranda's story: Nadine Gordimer and the literature of Empire', *Novel*, 18, 3 (Spring 1985), 227–42.

Heinemann, Margot. '*Burger's Daughter*: the synthesis of revelation', in Douglas Jefferson and Graham Martin (eds) *The Uses of Fiction*, Milton Keynes: Open University Press, 1982, pp. 181–97.

Holland, Roy. 'The critical writing of Nadine Gordimer', *Communiqué*, VII, 2 (1982), 7–33.

Hope, Christopher. 'Out of the picture: the novels of Nadine Gordimer', *London Magazine*, XV, 1 (1975), 49–55.

Laredo, Ursula. 'African mosaic: the novels of Nadine Gordimer', *Journal of Commonwealth Literature*, VIII, 1 (1973), 42–53.

Lomberg, Alan. 'Withering into the truth: the romantic realism of Nadine Gordimer', *English in Africa*, 3, 1 (1976), 1–12.

Ogungbesan, Kolawole. 'Nadine Gordimer's *The Late Bourgeois World*: love in prison', *Ariel*, 9, 1 (1978), 31–49.

Ogungbesan, Kolawole. 'Nadine Gordimer's *A Guest of Honour*: politics, fiction and the Liberal expatriate', *Southern Review*, 12 (1979), 180–223.

Rich, Paul. 'Tradition and revolt in South African fiction: the novels of André Brink, Nadine Gordimer and J. M. Coetzee', *Journal of Southern African Studies*, 9, 1 (1982), 54–73.

Roberts, Sheila. 'Nadine Gordimer's "family of women"', *Theoria*, LX (1983), 45–57.

Smith, Rowland. 'Living for the future: Nadine Gordimer's *Burger's Daughter*', *World Literature Written in English*, XIX (1980), 163–73.

Smyer, Richard I. 'Risk, frontier and interregnum in the fiction of Nadine Gordimer', *Journal of Commonwealth Literature*, XX, 1 (1985), 68–80.

Trump, Martin. 'The short fiction of Nadine Gordimer', *Research in African Literatures*, 17, 3 (1986), 341–69.

Wettenhall, Irene. 'Liberalism and radicalism in South Africa since 1948: Nadine Gordimer's fiction', *New Literature Review*, 8 (1980), 36–44.

2010
2013